MAGIC
MANDALA

A book of coloring in

By Lindy Longhurst

MAGIC MANDALA
A book of coloring in

Published by Blue Angel Publishing®
80 Glen Tower Drive, Glen Waverley
Victoria, Australia 3150
info@blueangelonline.com
blueangelonline.com

By Lindy Longhurst

Edited by Leela J. Williams

Blue Angel Publishing is a registered
trademark of Blue Angel Gallery Pty. Ltd.

ISBN: 978-1-922573-45-2

Circles of CREATION

Mandalas are interconnected, flowing, symbolic and spiritual images. Their many layers can be explored consciously and subconsciously, evoking the known and unknown within us. For this reason, they are often used as tools for introspection, healing and meditation.

I started drawing mandalas many years ago as a first step in reconnecting with my artistic expression. Having a circle to fill somehow made creating less daunting and enabled me to let go and see what evolved spontaneously and intuitively. Mandala making quickly became a flowing process that continues to help center me.

Nature inspires me, as do the elements and the spirit that flows through everything and connects us all. Shapes, patterns and colors combine within the mandalas, and I love how the elements weave together to create a many-layered story.

To begin, I created personalized mandalas for friends and family. Eventually, I moved into the different series, such as astrology, chakras, landscapes, tarot and fairy tales. I enjoyed revisiting each mandala and its themes to create the line drawings for this coloring book. I'm forever grateful that I had a chance to explore my creativity through mandala making, and I hope you find the same joy in coloring them.

Lindy

CONTENTS

These images are from the first series I created using mandalas. All twelve designs were completed within six weeks. It was an epic experience that was thoroughly inspired. The structure of each mandala, the colors, shapes, symbols and images are all connected to the individual zodiac sign.

This mandala series is based on chakras, the body's seven main energy centers. Kundalini energy, or serpent power, rises from below the root chakra at the base of the spine and makes its way up through each energy center to the crown chakra. Here it unites with the all-pervading power of the Universe. When the chakras are balanced, there is a clear path through which kundalini can flow and foster more peace, satisfaction, joy and balance within us.

Australian landscapes have always inspired me. It was a great experience to travel the country and see the many different landscapes and animals of this continent. This series is devoted to imagery from my travels.

Each of these mandalas depicts the entire story of a well-known fairy tale.

Consisting of twenty-two images, the Major Arcana of the Tarot represents a journey of the self from The Fool to The World. The fifty-six cards of the Minor Arcana describe more everyday interactions and are broken up into four suits: cups (water/emotions), wands (fire/activity), coins (earth/practicality, material life) and swords (air/mental activity).

Personal mandalas are tools for introspection, growth and healing. They combine conscious and subconscious elements of an individual, group, or couple's life to craft a unique story based on the past, present and future. Each mandala in this section was created spontaneously and uniquely for the individual.

ARIES

March 21 – April 19

Symbol: Ram

Element: Fire

Planet: Mars

In nature: Volcanos, stars, bushfires

Animals: The Ram

Mandala form: Fast movement, explosive enthusiasm

Qualities: Childlike enthusiasm, spontaneity, freshness, independence, initiative, leadership abilities, headfirst into situations, need for constant activity, raw energy.

Wax-based pencils, gouache and oil pastels on paper 50 x 50cm

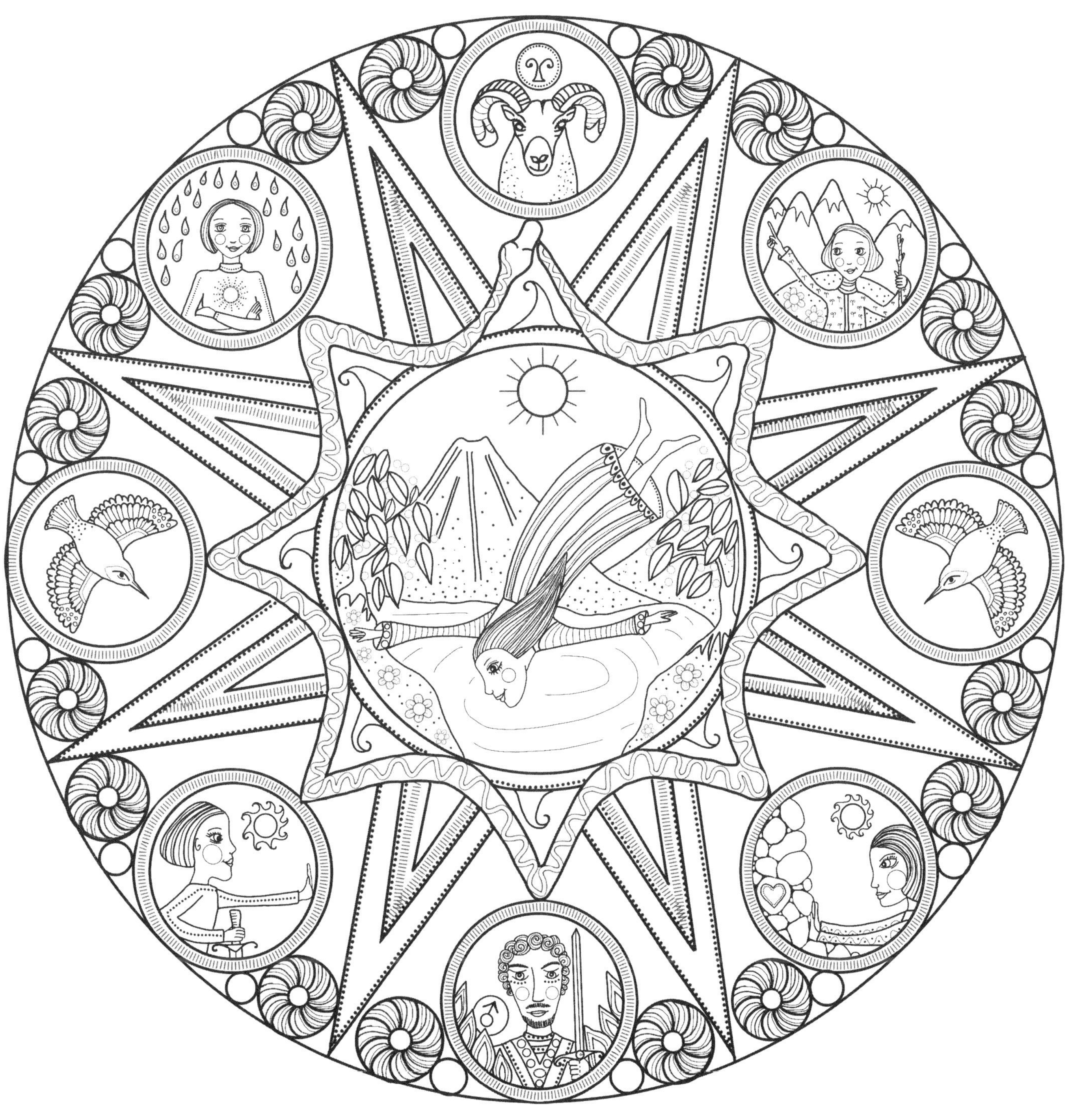

TAURUS

◆

April 20 – May 20

Symbol: Bull

Element: Earth

Planet: Venus

In nature: Mountains, wood

Animals: Bulls, cows

Mandala form: Solid, secure, natural abundance

Qualities: Security, stability, persevering strength,
determination, patience, reliability, dependability,
family connections, love, sensuality, pleasure,
material needs, accumulation, storage and saving.

Wax-based pencils, gouache and oil pastels on paper 50 x 50cm

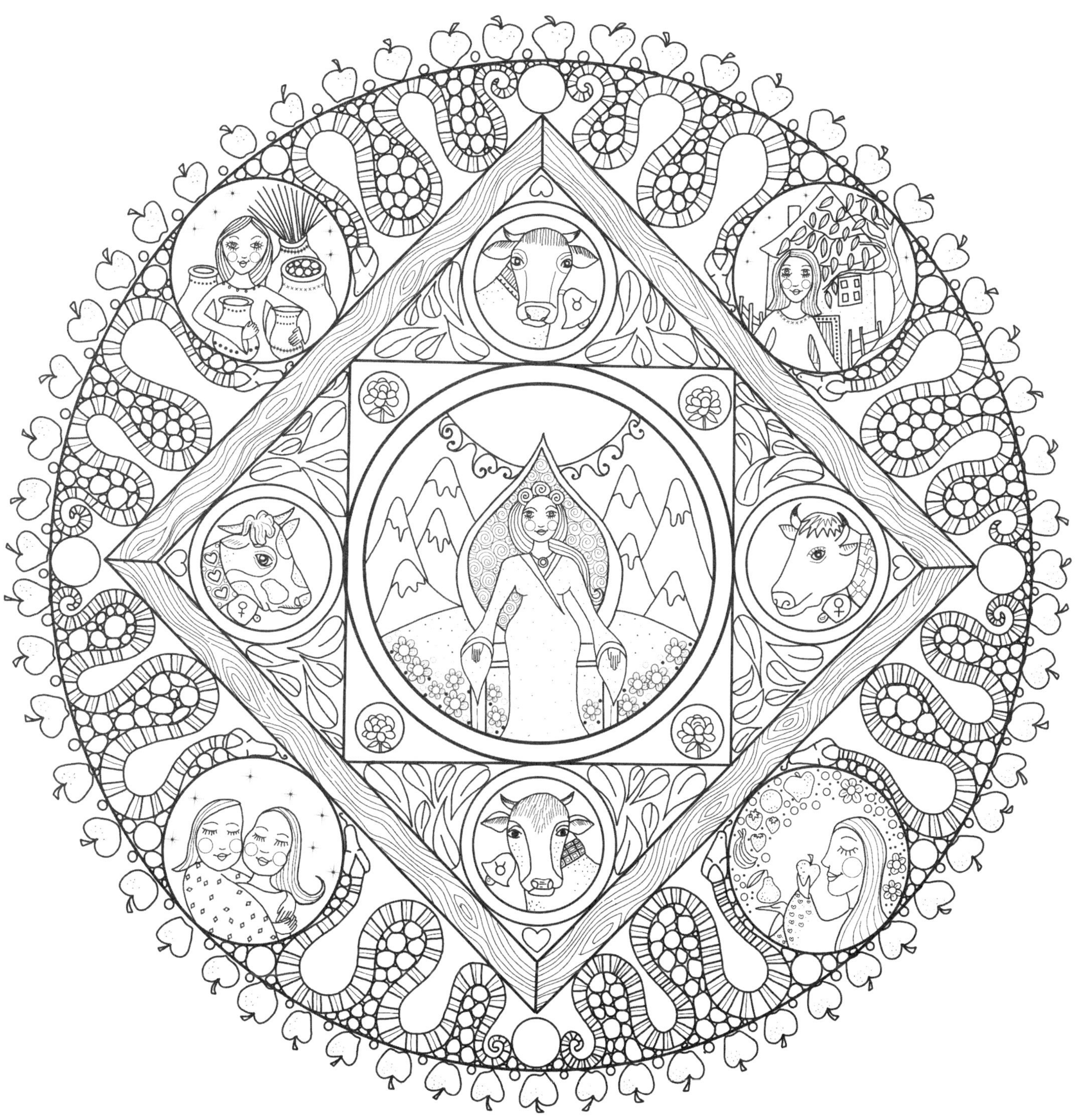

GEMINI

May 21 – June 20

Symbol: Twins

Element: Air

Planet: Mercury

In nature: Breezes, whirlwinds

Animals: Chittering colorful birds, small flying creatures

Mandala form: Busy movement, variety,
diversity, magical, fairylike

Qualities: Talkative, communicative, excitable, sociable, love
of diversity, variety, activity, rapid movement, information
gathering, knowledge, quick intellect, curiosity, interest, wit.

Wax-based pencils, gouache and oil pastels on paper 50 x 50cm

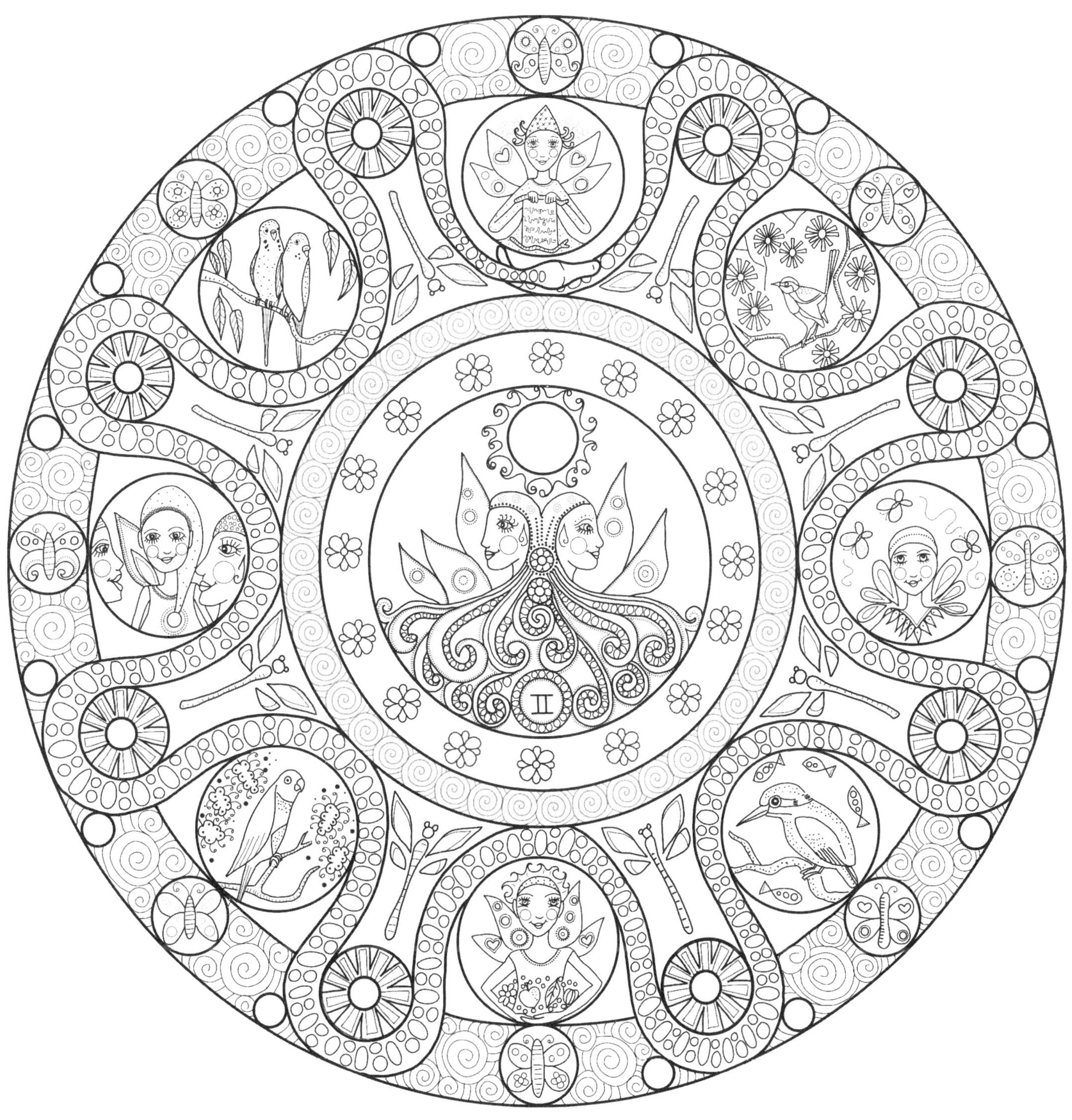

CANCER

◆

June 21 – July 22

Symbol: Crab

Element: Water

Planet: The Moon

In nature: The sea, protected waterways, estuaries, rivers

Animals: Crabs, crustaceans, tortoises, sea mammals

Mandala form: Nurturing, flowing, protective, soft

Qualities: Intuitive, changeable, emotional, self-protecting, need for security, nurturing, deep attachment with others, loving, keeper of all things cherished and sentimental, the 'mother' of the zodiac.

Wax-based pencils, gouache and oil pastels on paper 50 x 50cm

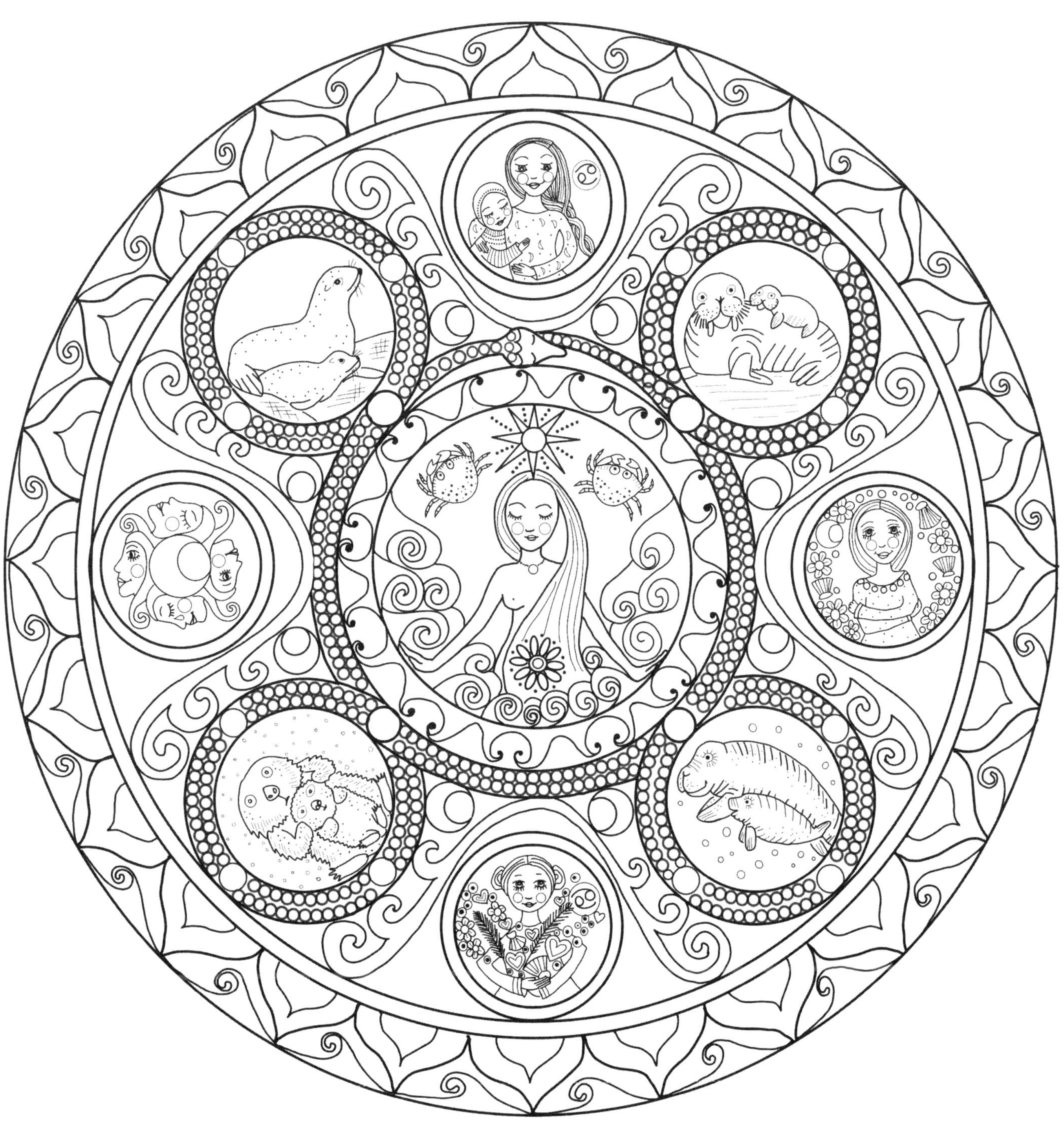

LEO

♦

July 23 – August 22

Symbol: Lion

Element: Fire

Planet: The Sun

In nature: The Sun

Animals: Big cats, dragons

Mandala form: Regal, fixed, dynamic

Qualities: Flamboyant, energetic, enthusiastic, loyal, faithful, big-hearted, childlike, generous, affectionate, creative, dramatic, expressive, strong, courageous, leadership.

Wax-based pencils, gouache and oil pastels on paper 50 x 50cm

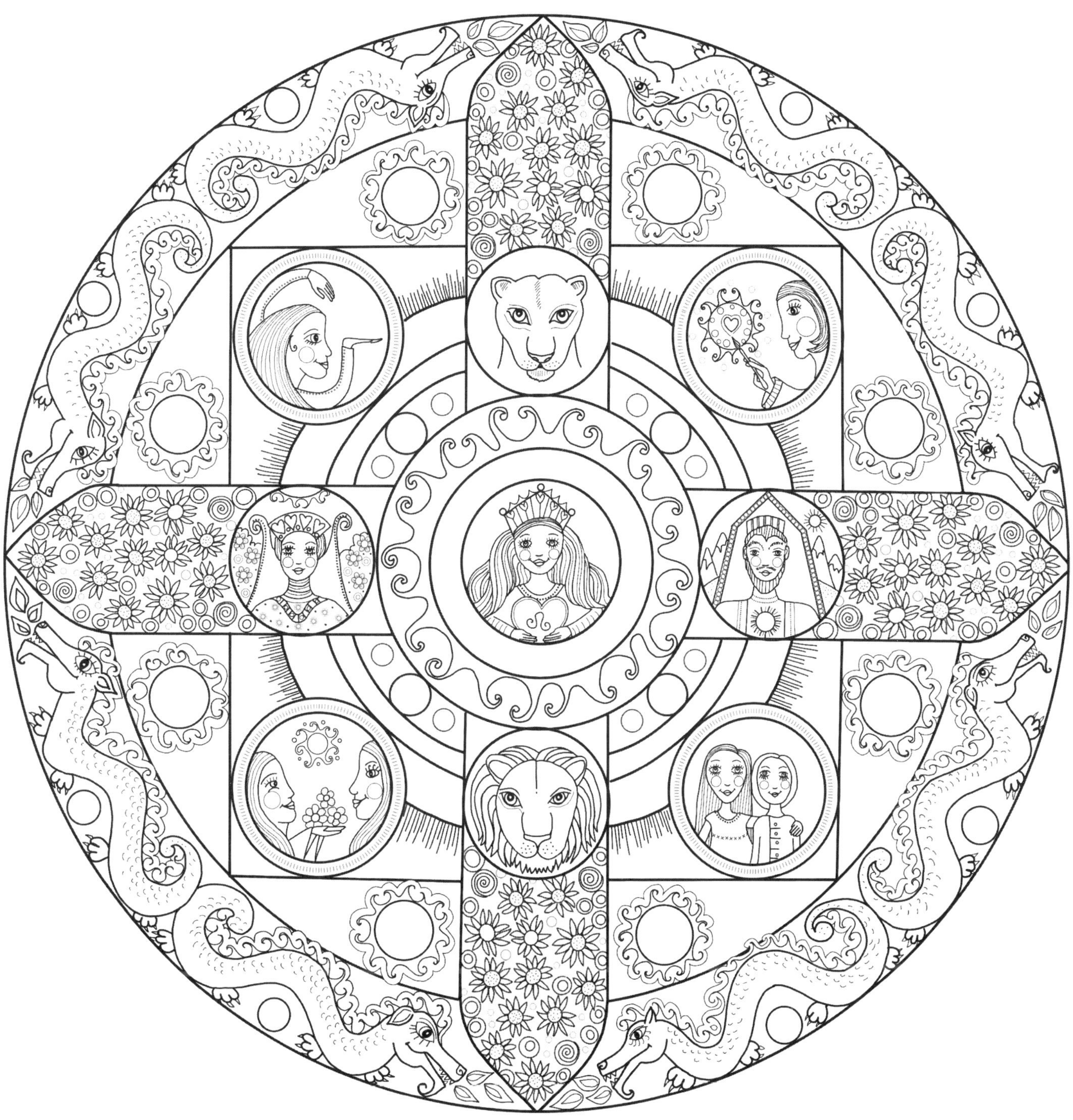

VIRGO

August 23 – September 22

Symbol: The Virgin/Earth Goddess

Element: Earth

Planet: Mercury

In nature: Earth, flowers, the change of seasons

Animals: Small burrowing animals

Mandala form: Structured, soft and feminine

Qualities: Love of detail, precision, organized,
particular, observant, analytical, versatile, desire
for perfection, completion and wholeness.

Wax-based pencils, gouache and oil pastels on paper 50 x 50cm

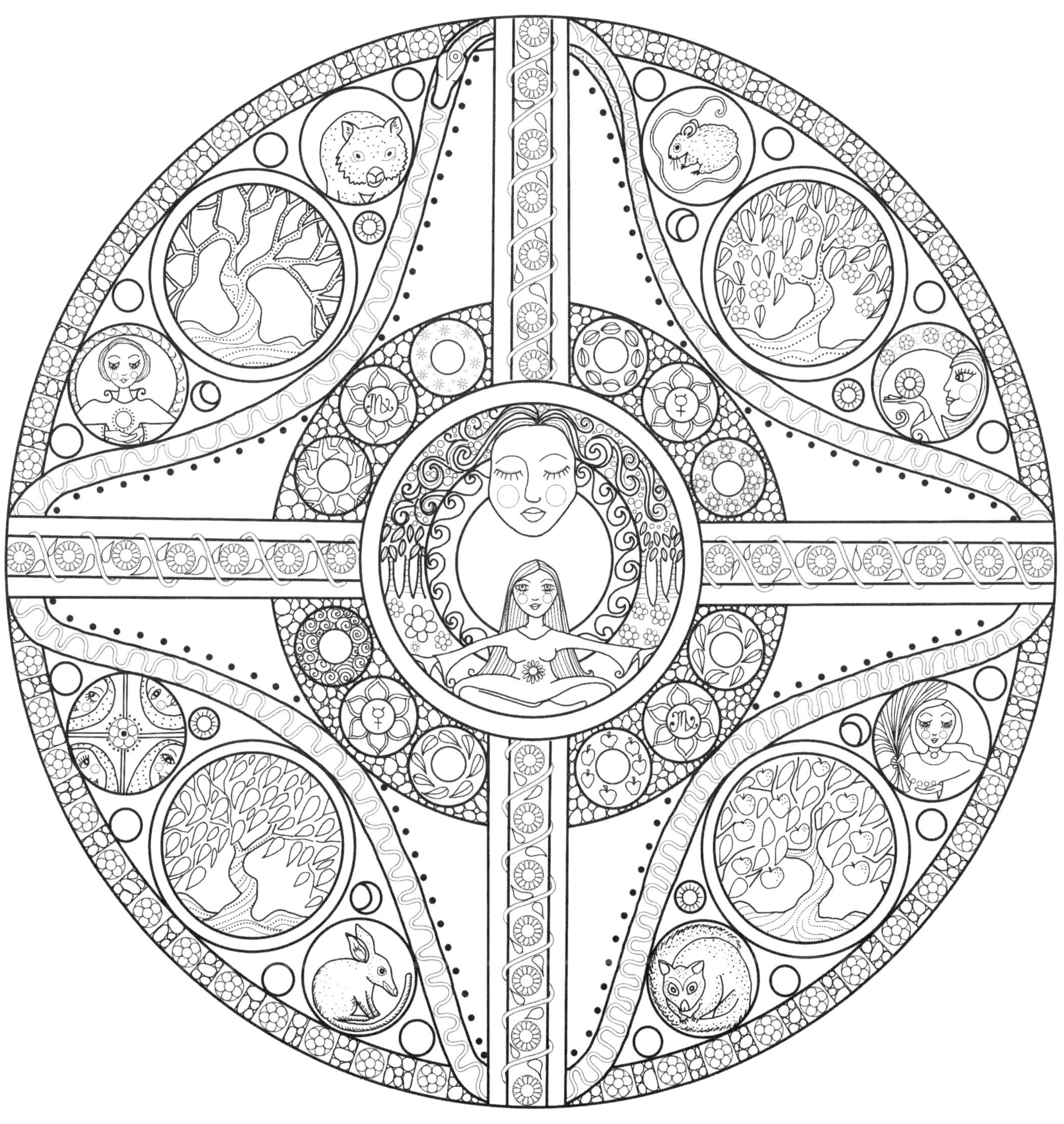

LIBRA

◆

September 23 – October 22

Symbol: Scales

Element: Air

Planet: Venus

In nature: Clear skies, soft breezes

Animals: Elephants, reptiles

Mandala form: Soft, pretty, harmonious

Qualities: Balanced, diplomatic, fair, just, keeper of calm,
peaceful, harmonious, loving, romantic, idealistic,
a love of all things fine, grace, elegance, beauty.

Wax-based pencils, gouache and oil pastels on paper 50 x 50cm

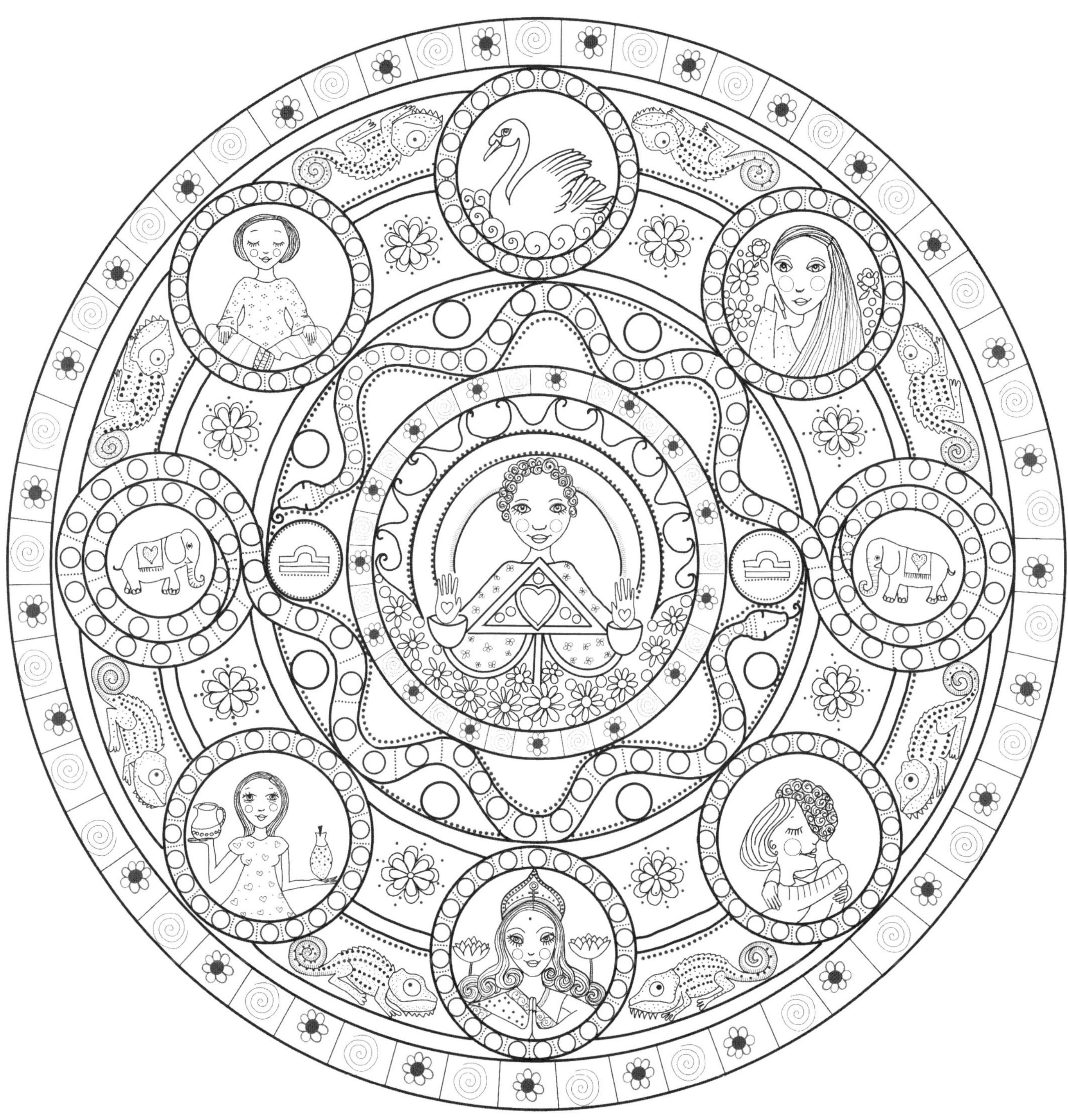

SCORPIO

◆

October 23 – November 21

Symbol: Scorpion

Element: Water

Planets: Mars and Pluto

In nature: Deep pools, dark forests

Animals: Eagles, wolves, owls, scorpions

Mandala form: Inwardly focused, coiled tension

Qualities: Emotional intensity, depth, regeneration, perception, awareness of undercurrents, passion, dedication, desire, personal power, magnetism, wisdom, strength, protection of themselves and loved ones.

Wax-based pencils, gouache and oil pastels on paper 50 x 50cm

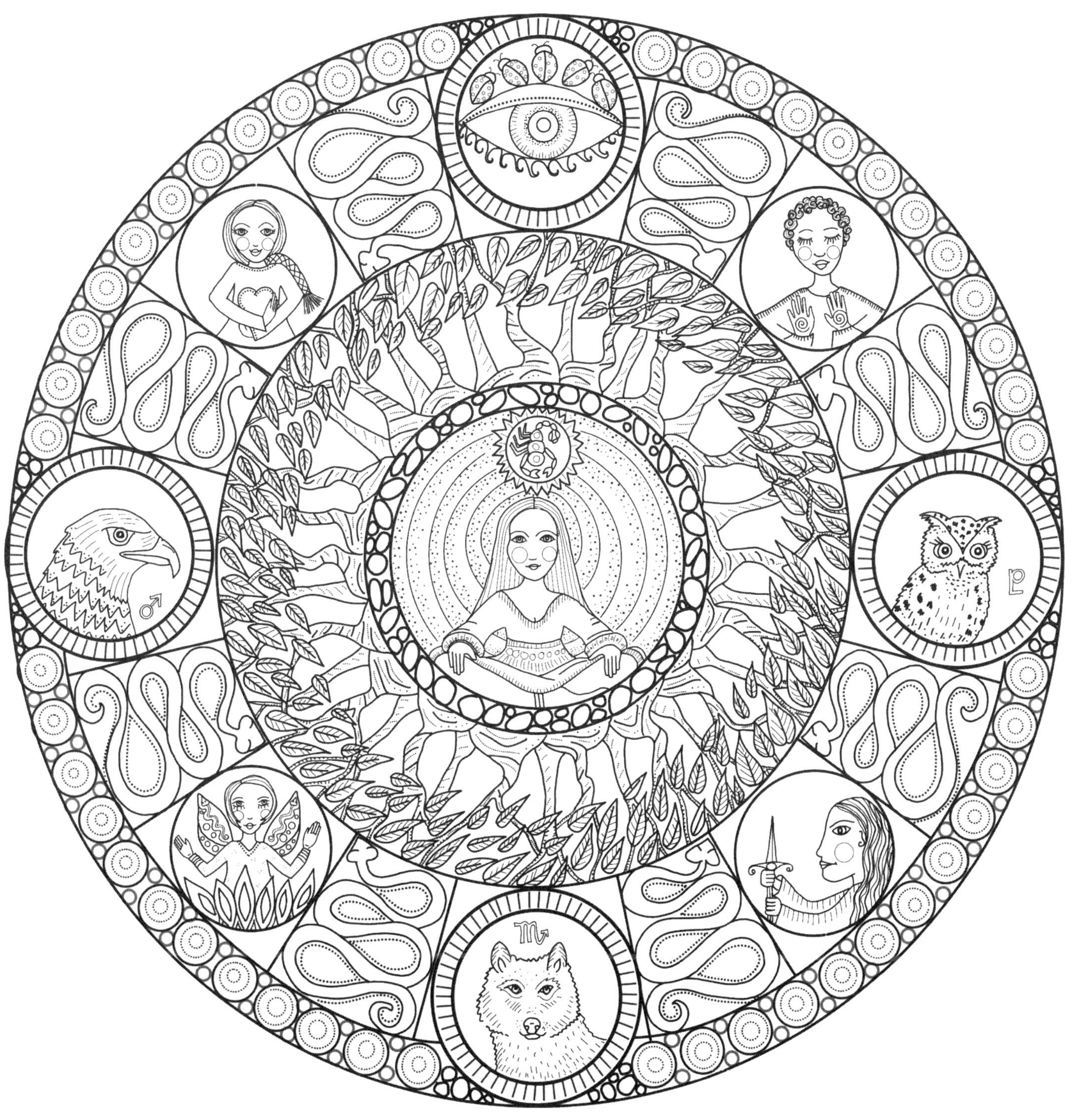

SAGITTARIUS

November 22 – December 21

Symbol: Archer/Centaur

Element: Fire

Planet: Jupiter

In nature: Open spaces, the night sky

Animals: Horses, unicorns, Pegasus, dogs

Mandala form: Open, expansive

Qualities: Physical and spiritual travel, adventurer, love of freedom, openness, honesty, interest in philosophy, culture and spirituality, broad outlook on life and the universe.

Wax-based pencils, gouache and oil pastels on paper 50 x 50cm

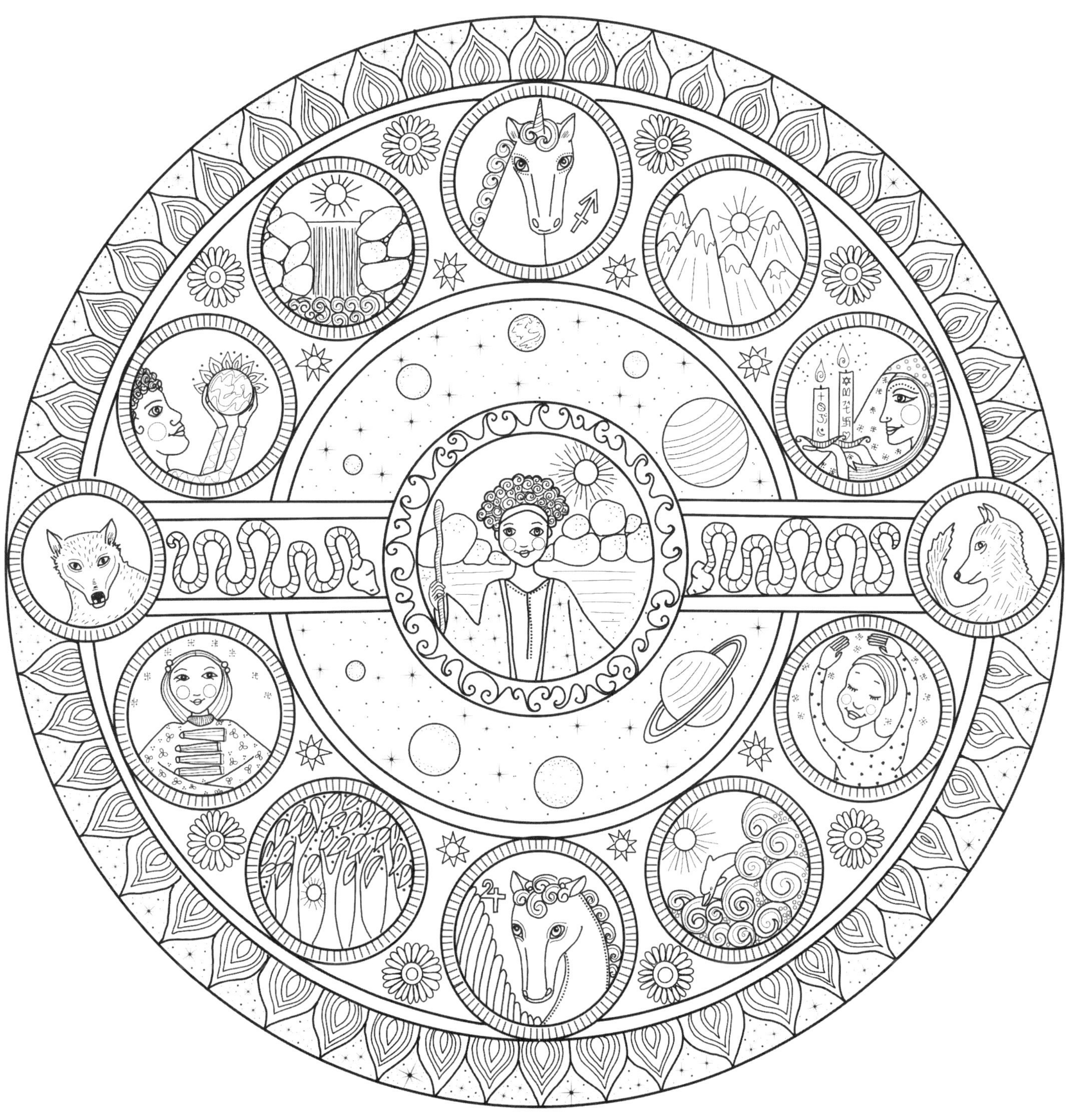

CAPRICORN

◆

December 22 – January 19

Symbol: Goat

Element: Earth

Planet: Saturn

In nature: Soil, leaves, fruits, products of the earth

Animals: Goats

Mandala form: Organized, structured, earthy

Qualities: Organized, disciplined, ready to work,
ambitious, prepared, foresighted, focused, practical,
independent, constant, sees things through to the end.

Wax-based pencils, gouache and oil pastels on paper 50 x 50cm

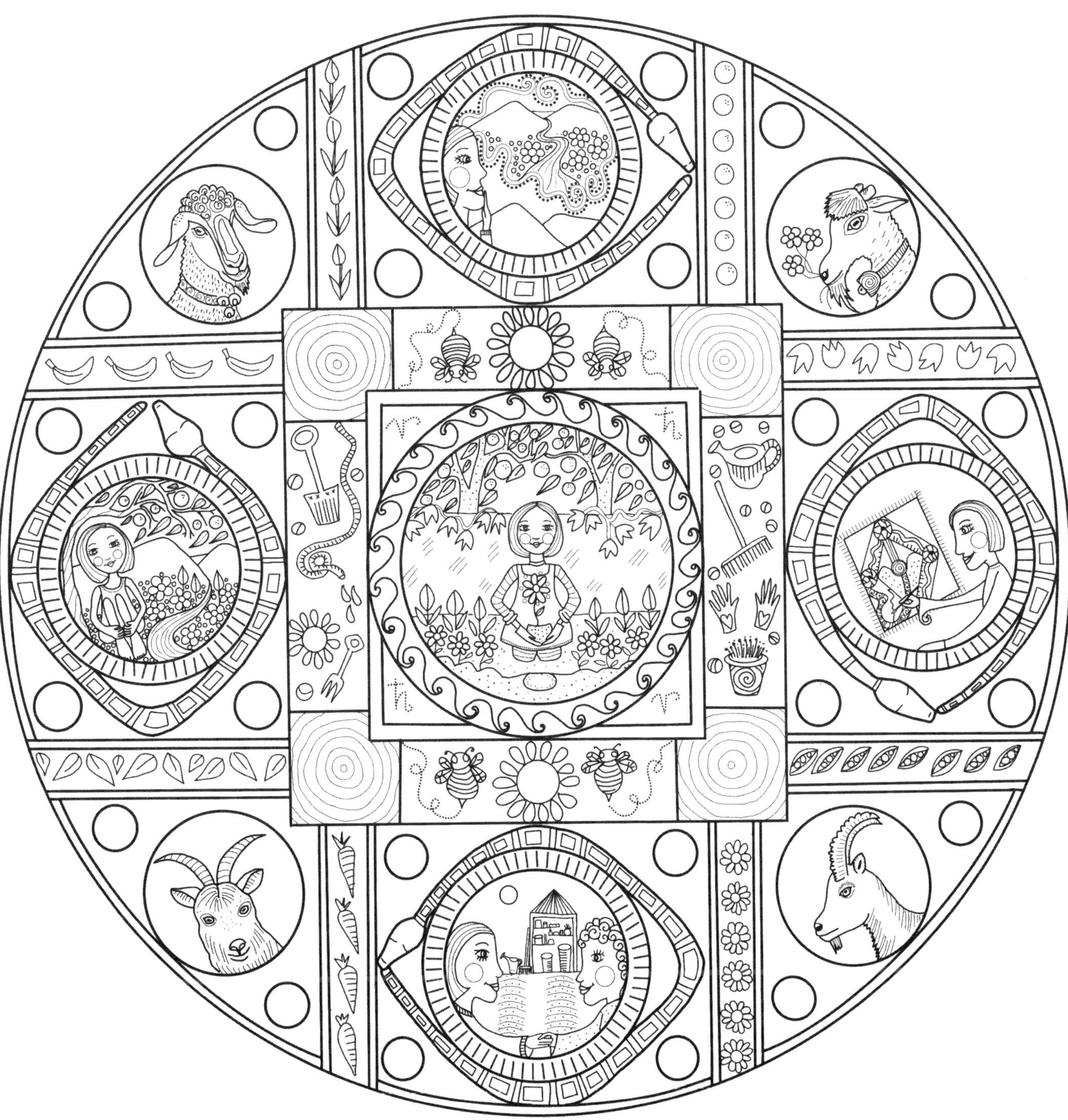

AQUARIUS

♦

January 20 – February 18

Symbol: Water Bearer

Element: Air

Planet: Uranus

In nature: The sky, weather patterns, clouds, lightning

Animals: Large birds, long flying

Mandala form: Inorganic structure, constructed

Qualities: Intelligence, abstract thinking, science, technology, invention, diplomacy, humanitarian, open but aloof, eccentric, sporadic, independent, original, honest, idealistic.

Wax-based pencils, gouache and oil pastels on paper 50 x 50cm

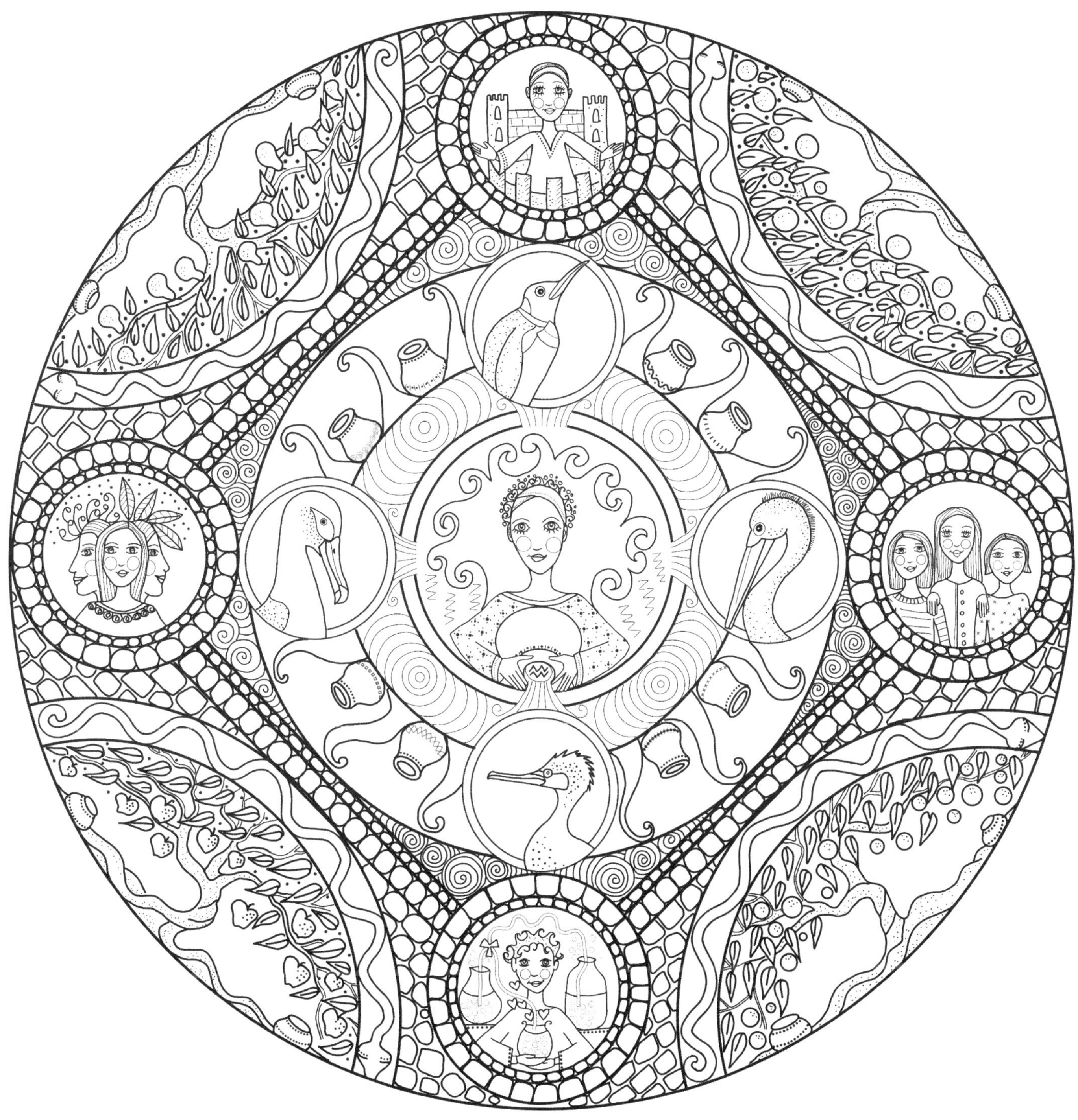

PISCES

◆

February 19 – March 20

Symbol: Fish/Mermaid

Element: Water

Planet: Neptune

In nature: Deep sea

Animals: Fish, sea creatures

Mandala form: Soft, flowing, dreamy

Qualities: Intuitive, receptive to hidden worlds, in touch with the subconscious, dreamy, compassionate, caring, soulful, sensitive, imaginative, desire for union, completion, knowledge of the unknown.

Wax-based pencils, gouache and oil pastels on paper 50 x 50cm

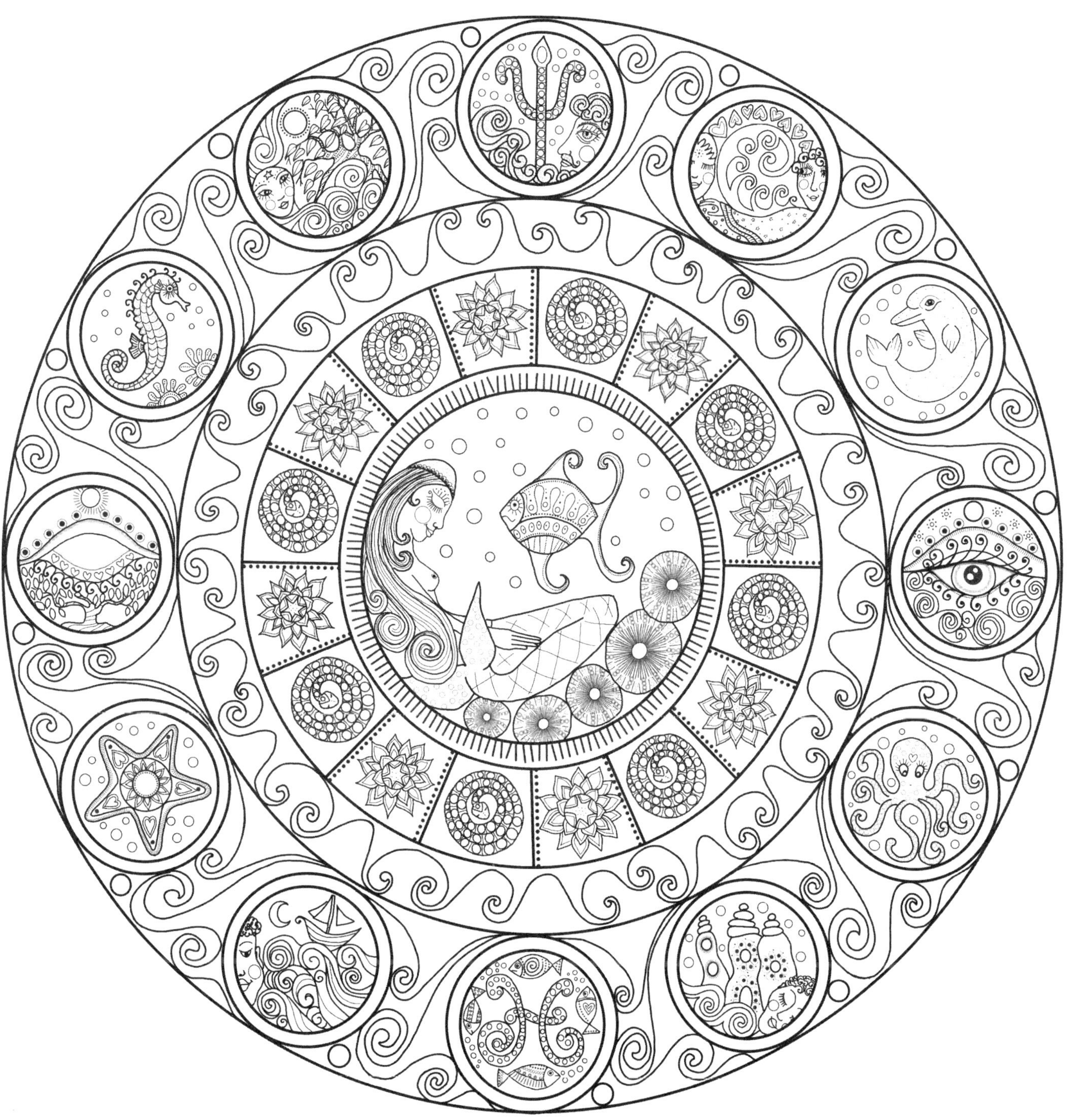

THE FIRST CHAKRA

◆

Mooladhara/Root/Base Chakra

Seed mantra: Lam

Element: Earth

Color: Red

Location: Base of the spine

Deity: Ganesha

Symbol: Four-petaled lotus

Qualities: Innocence, wisdom, simplicity, joy, integrity, survival, passion, loyalty, animal instinct. Kundalini energy lies dormant in the sacrum bone beneath the first chakra until it is awakened.

Wax-based pencils, gouache and oil pastels on paper 50 x 50cm

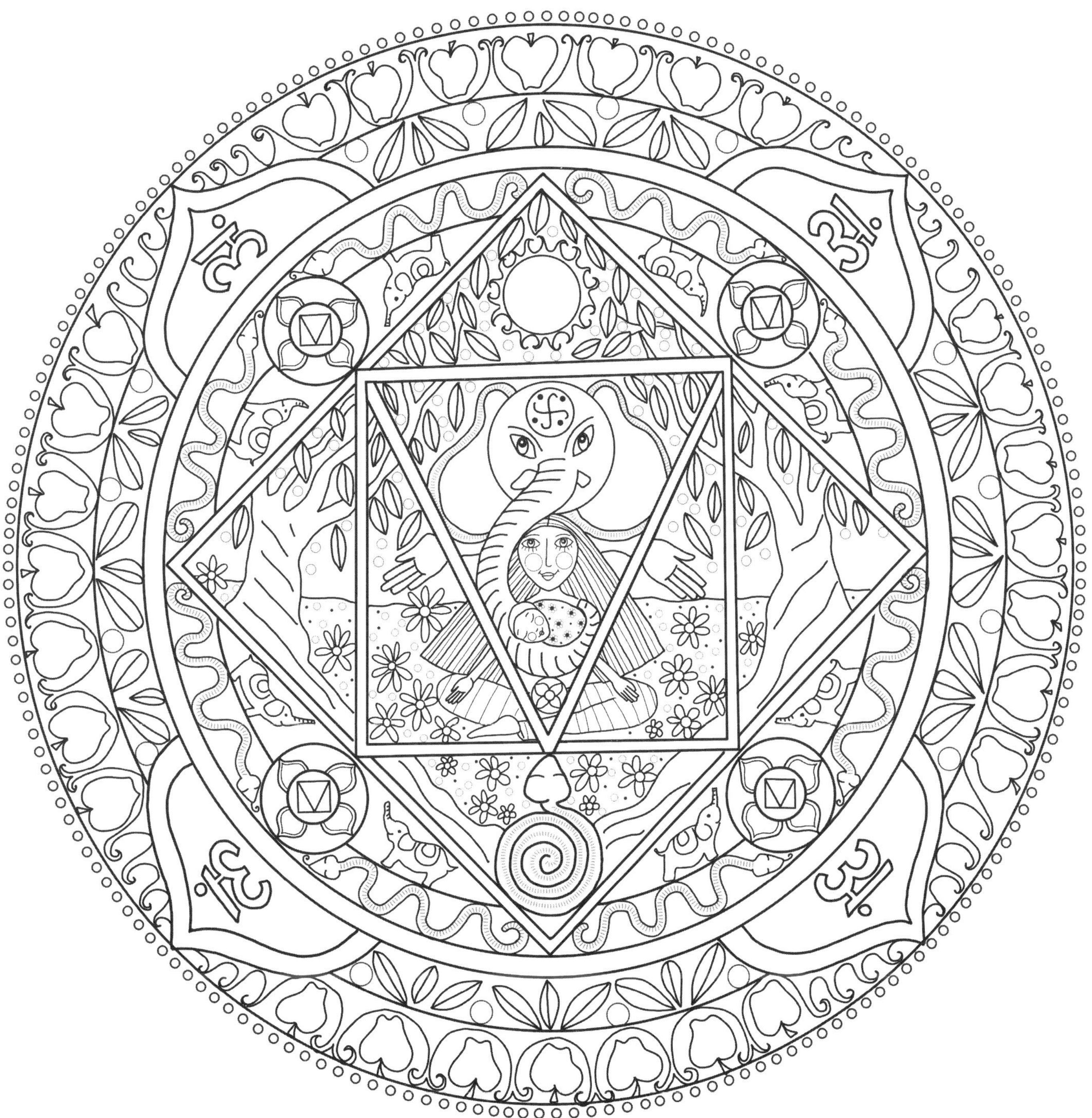

THE SECOND CHAKRA

Swadhistana/Sacral Chakra

Seed mantra: Vam

Element: Water

Color: Orange

Location: Below the navel

Deities: Brahma and Saraswati

Symbol: Six-petaled lotus

Qualities: Creativity, spontaneity, inspiration and
pure knowledge.

Wax-based pencils, gouache and oil pastels on paper 50 x 50cm

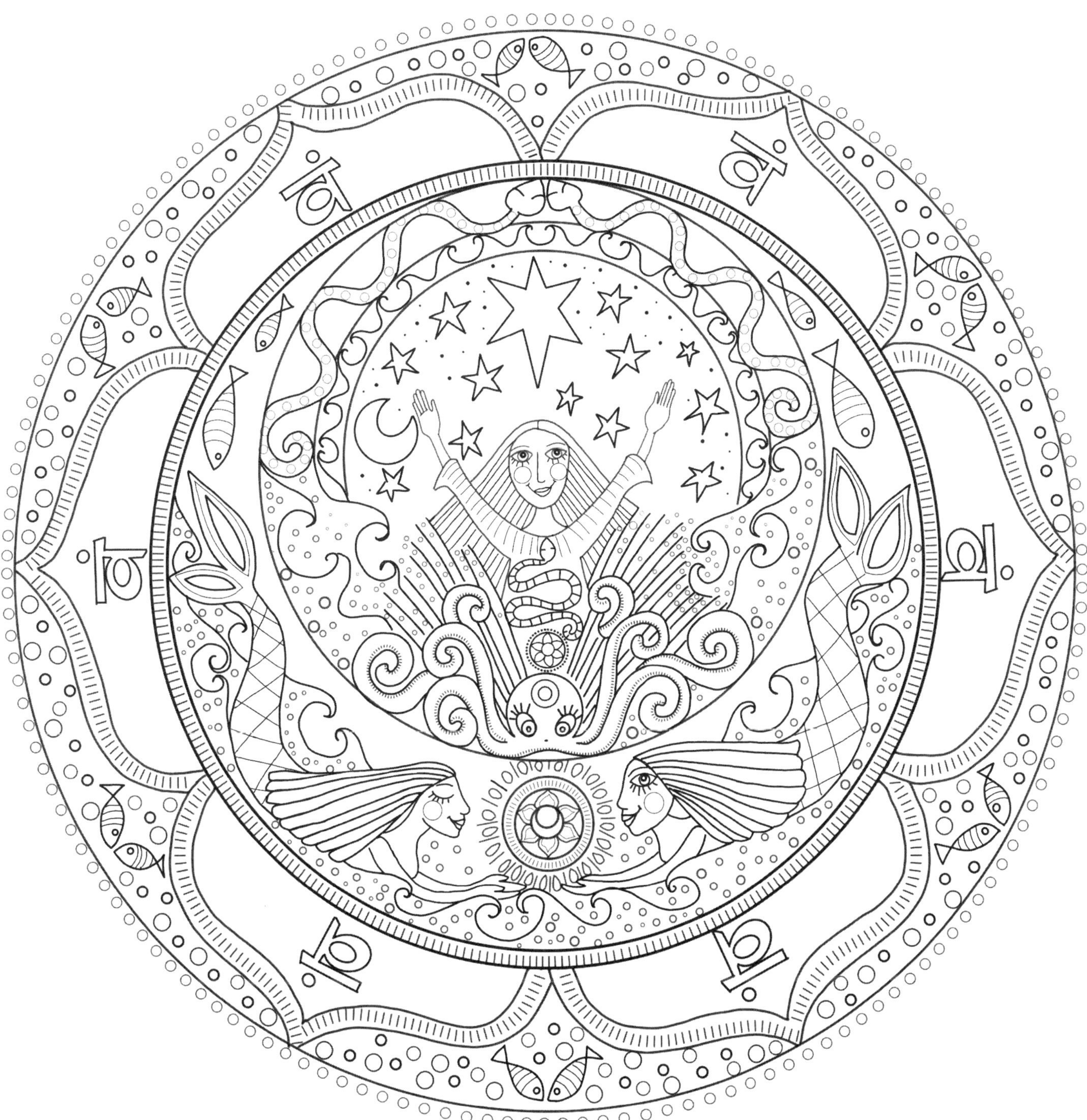

THE THIRD CHAKRA

◆

Nahbi/Solar Plexus Chakra

Seed mantra: Ram

Element: Fire

Color: Yellow

Location: Above the navel

Deities: Vishnu and Lakshmi

Symbol: Ten-petaled lotus

Qualities: Peace, wellbeing, contentment, satisfaction, generosity, purpose. Physical, material and spiritual sustenance.

Wax-based pencils, gouache and oil pastels on paper 50 x 50cm

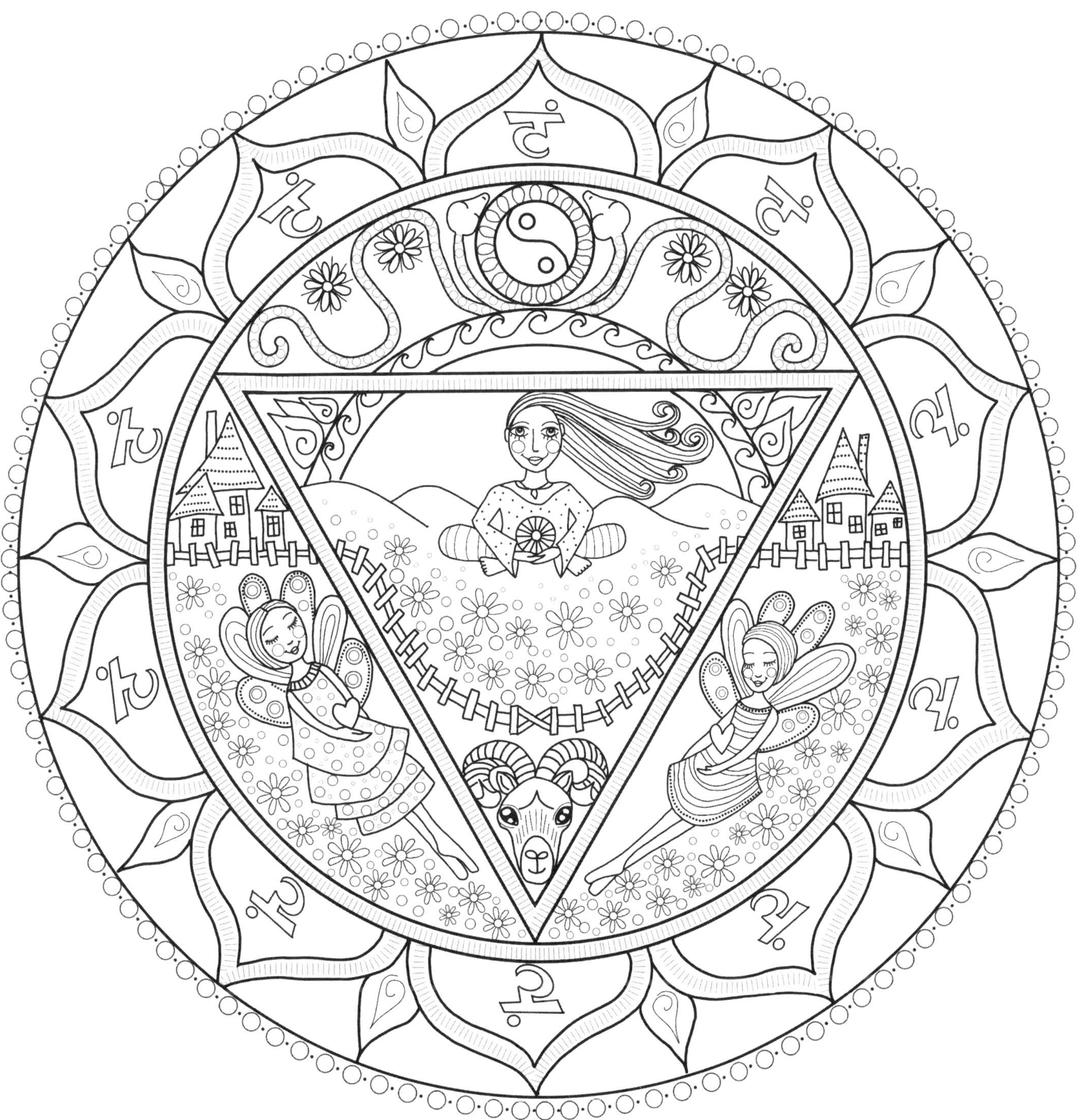

THE FOURTH CHAKRA

◆

Anahata/Heart Chakra

Seed mantra: Yam

Element: Air

Color: Green

Location: Heart

Deities: Siva and Parvati

Symbols: Twelve-petaled lotus. The hexagram inside represents the integration of masculine and feminine qualities.

Qualities: Unconditional love, truth, faith, joy, security, courage, loyalty, strength, fearlessness. The seat of the spirit — the eternal true self.

Wax-based pencils, gouache and oil pastels on paper 50 x 50cm

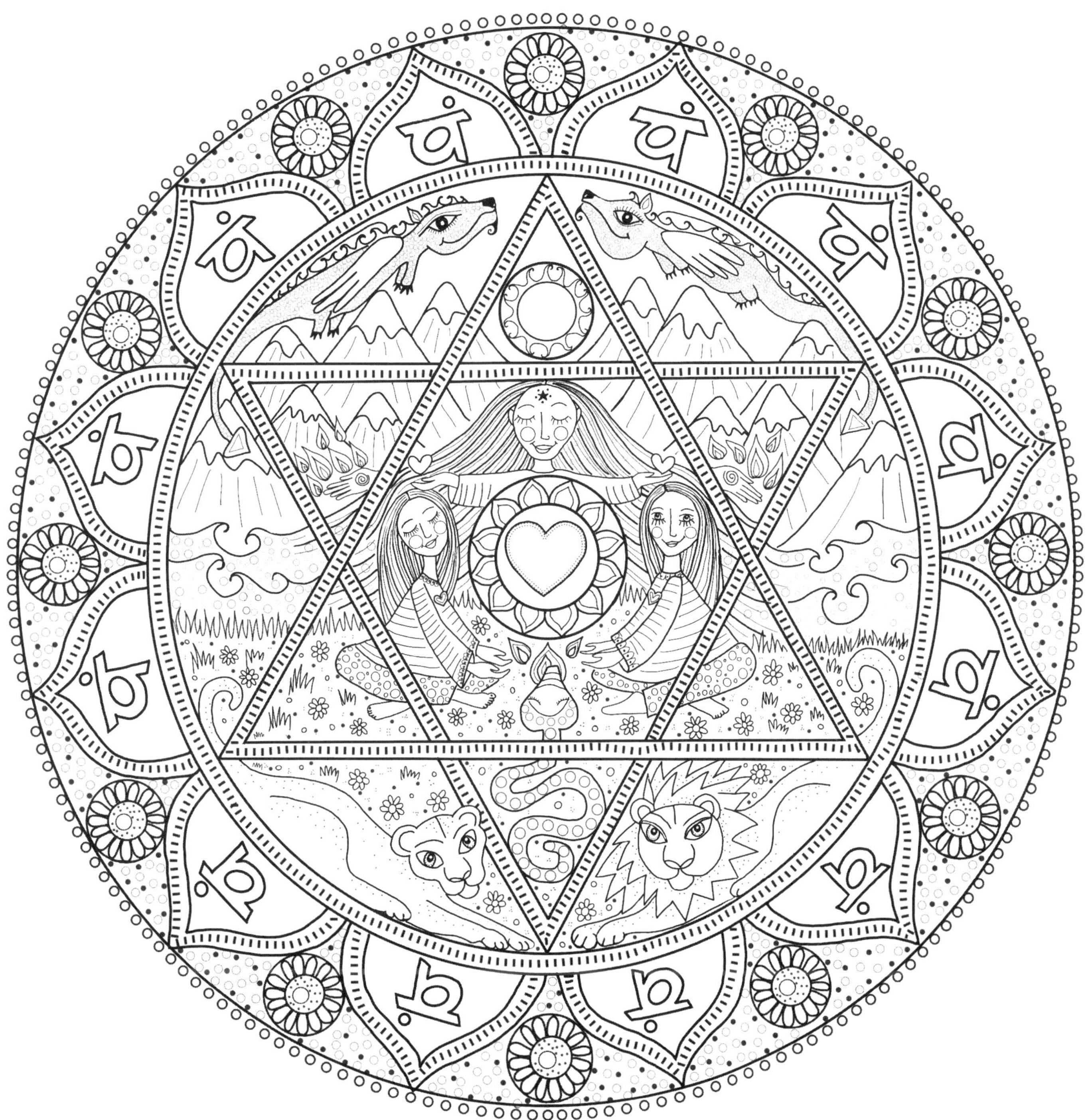

THE FIFTH CHAKRA

Vishuddhi/Throat Chakra

Seed mantra: Ham

Element: Ether

Color: Blue

Location: Throat

Deities: Radha and Krishna

Symbol: Sixteen-petaled lotus

Qualities: Diplomacy, truth, communication,
collective consciousness, detachment.

Wax-based pencils, gouache and oil pastels on paper 50 x 50cm

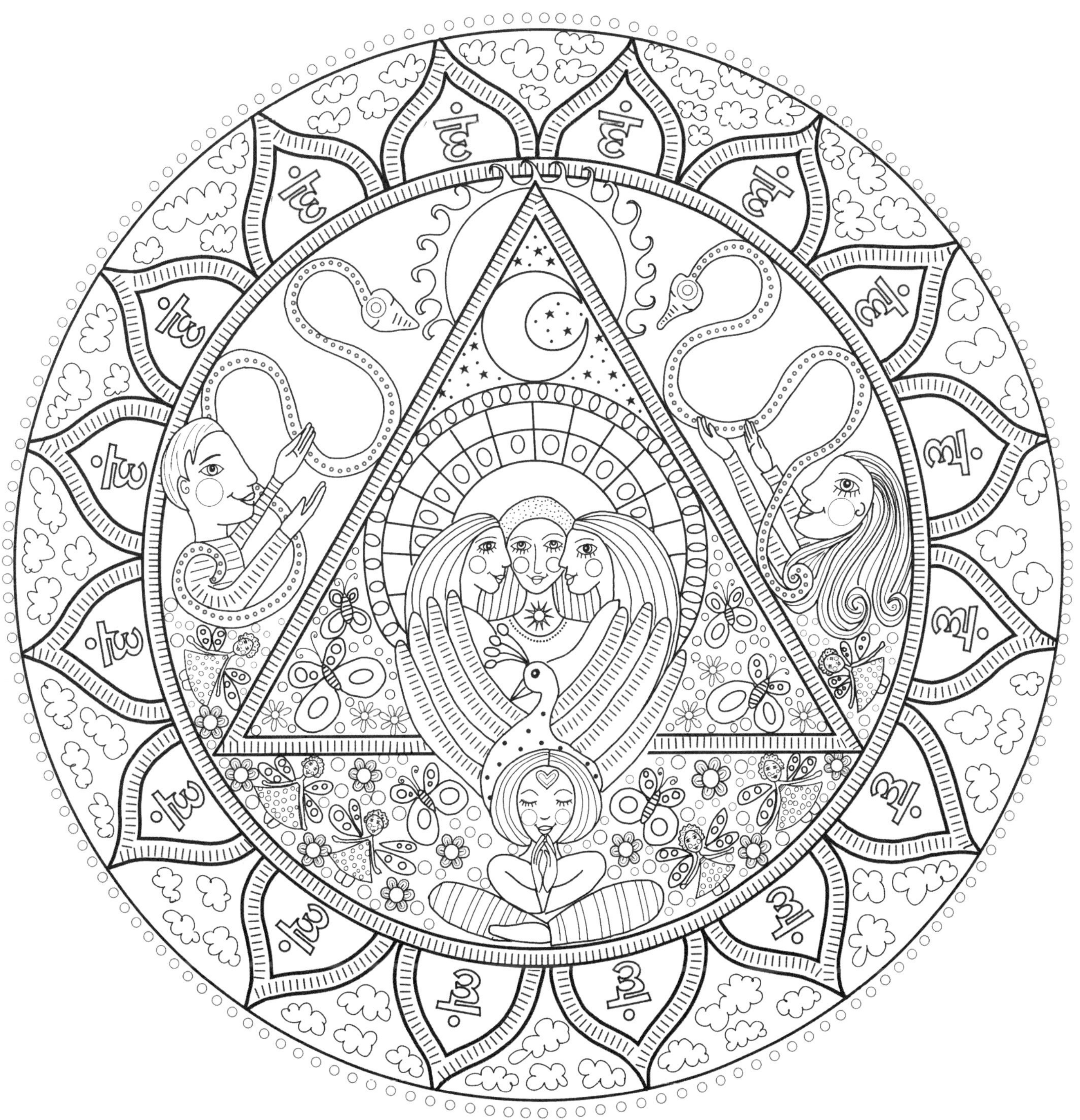

THE SIXTH CHAKRA

Agnya/Third Eye Chakra

Seed mantra: Aum

Element: Light

Color: Indigo/purple

Location: Forehead

Deities: Buddha and Jesus

Symbol: Two-petaled lotus

Qualities: Forgiveness, compassion, intuition,
awareness, clarity, higher consciousness.

Wax-based pencils, gouache and oil pastels on paper 50 x 50cm

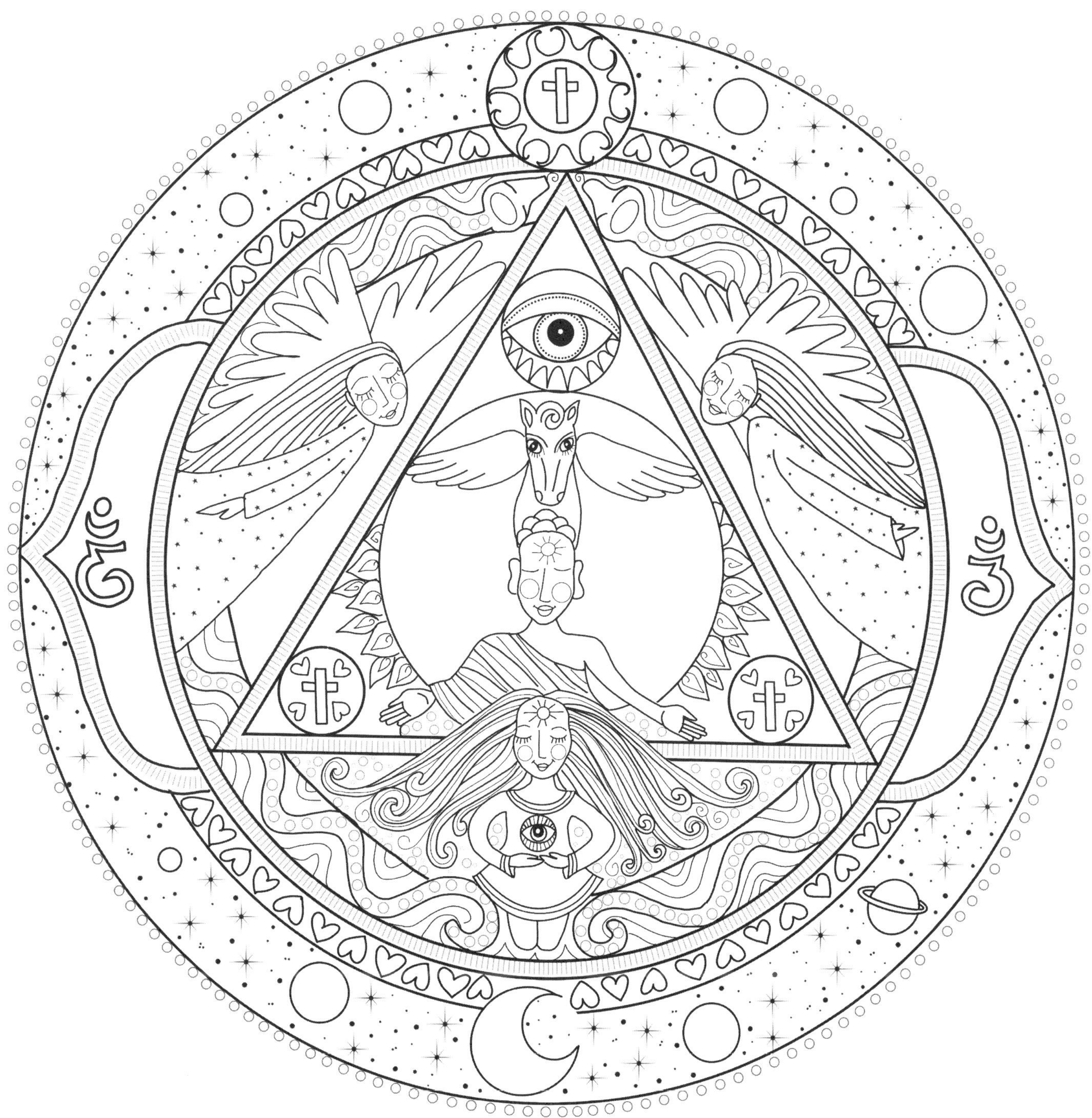

THE SEVENTH CHAKRA

Sahasrara/Crown Chakra

Seed mantra: Aum

Element: Pure spirit

Color: All colors/violet

Location: Crown

Deity: Shakti and Siva

Symbol: Thousand-petaled lotus

Qualities: Union, peace, integration, kundalini.
Knowledge beyond intellect. Connection with all that is.

Wax-based pencils, gouache and oil pastels on paper 50 x 50cm

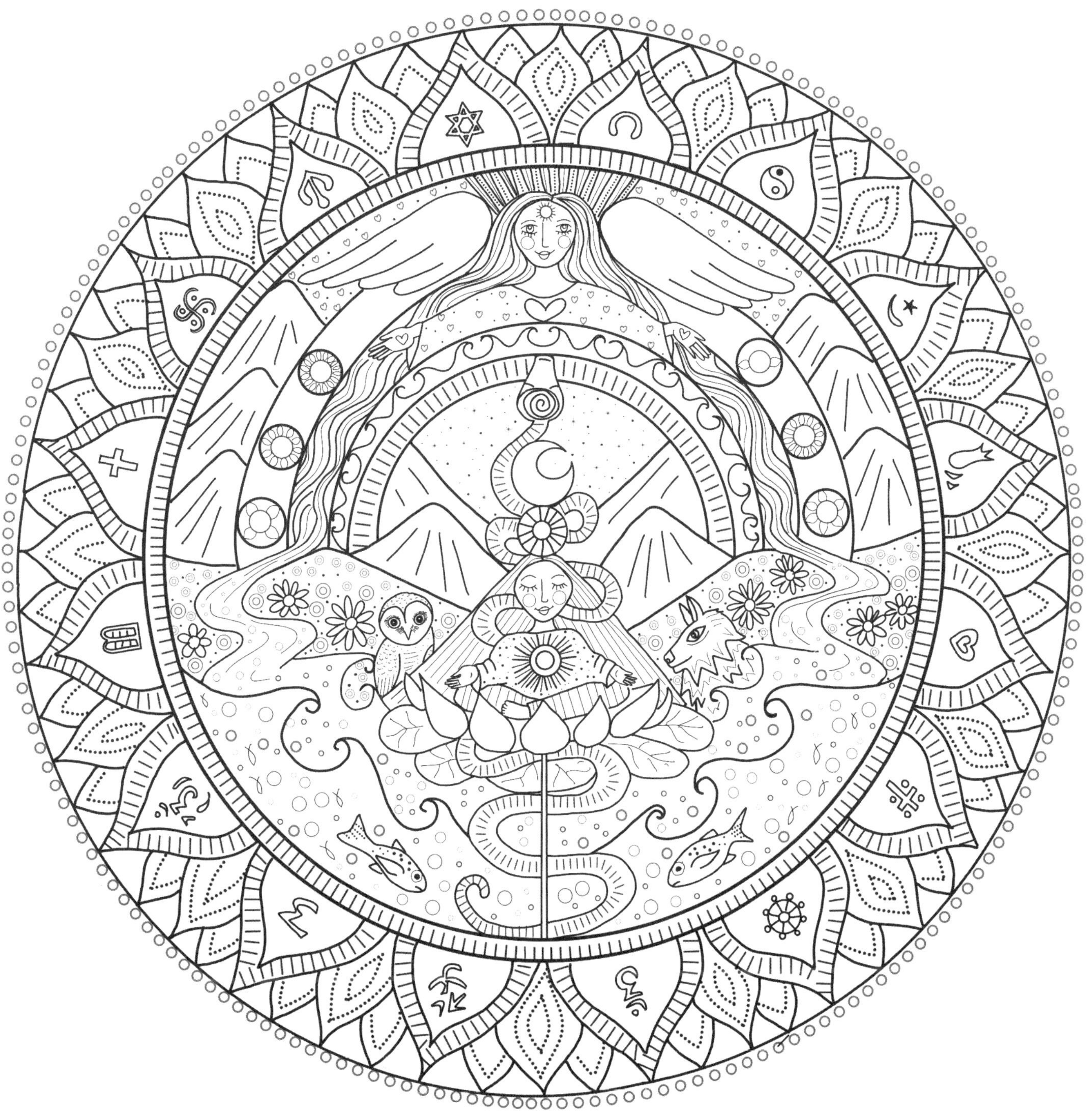

WILDFLOWERS

◆

Inspired by Australian birdlife and native flowers, this mandala has the sun at its center. It is surrounded by flannel flowers, wax flowers, butterflies and banksias. The mandala's structure incorporates circles for flow and a central rotated square to represent earth. Grevillea, wattle and waratahs surround the square. A serpent weaves around the edge to tie the elements together. The outer circle features well-known Australian birds. This was a bright and lively colored mandala to create.

Wax-based pencils, gouache and oil pastels on paper 50 x 50cm

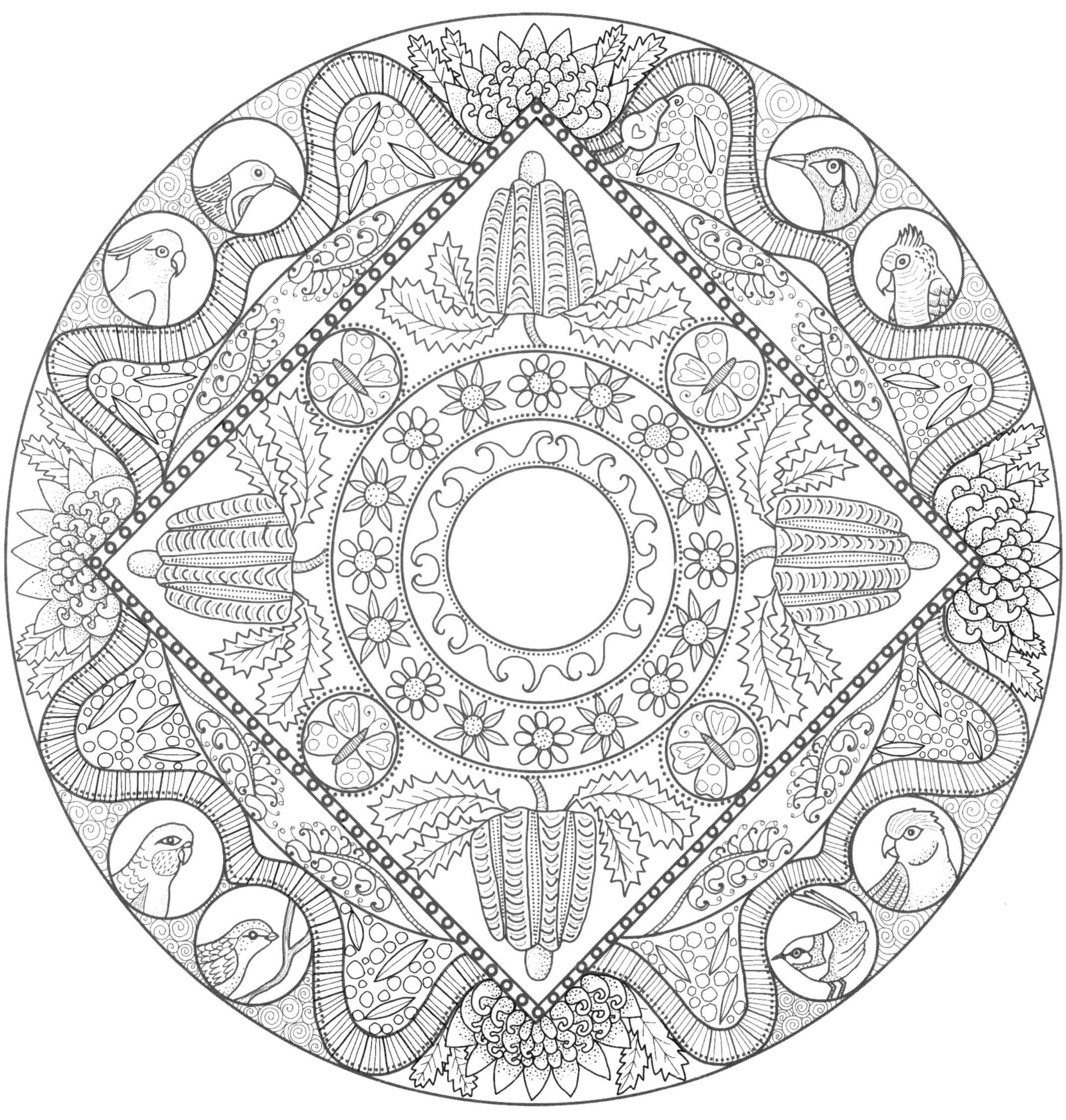

BUSHLAND, FOREST, SCRUB

Following the theme of the Australian bush, this mandala incorporates grasses, shrubs, eucalyptus trees, rivers, stones and mountains. The animals included are native to Australia and can be found in a variety of these landscapes. The serpent again forms part of the mandala to weave the elements together. The sun and moon make their presence, as both are essential to the ongoing cycle of diurnal and nocturnal animals. I kept the color palette quite earthy for this mandala.

Wax-based pencils, gouache and oil pastels on paper 50 x 50cm

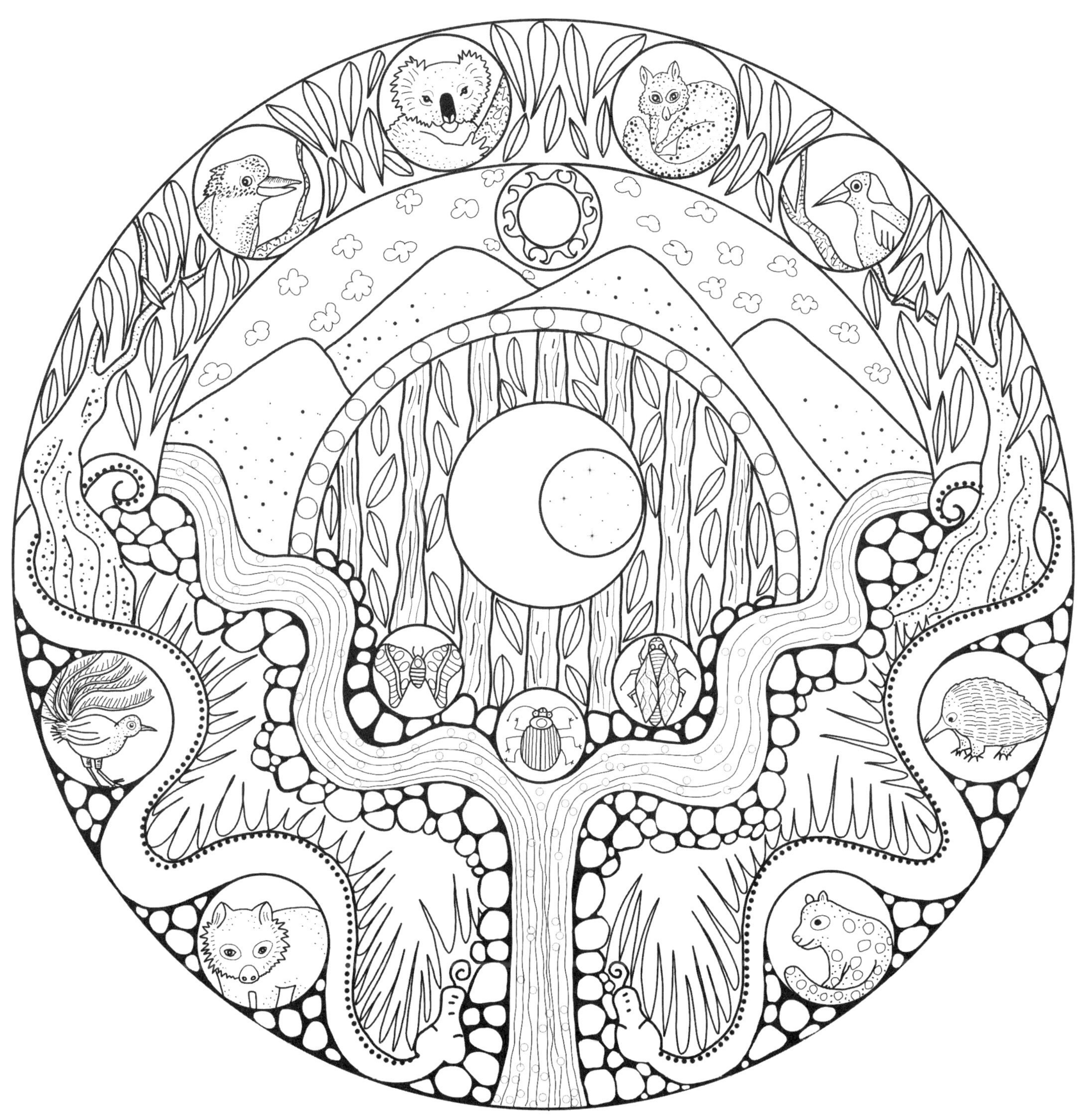

RAINFOREST

◆

I wanted to create the feeling of immersion, like being in the thick of a rainforest. I used a limited and darker color palette and placed the trees close together. Once again, the animals are native to Australia. A butterfly is in the center, surrounded by a sun. The mandala then flows into vegetation and water, with trees reaching from the edges to the center. Roots, soil, vines, leaves and flowers also feature as part of the overall ecosystem of the rainforest. The serpent weaves around on the rainforest floor bringing the elements together.

Wax-based pencils, gouache and oil pastels on paper 50 x 50cm

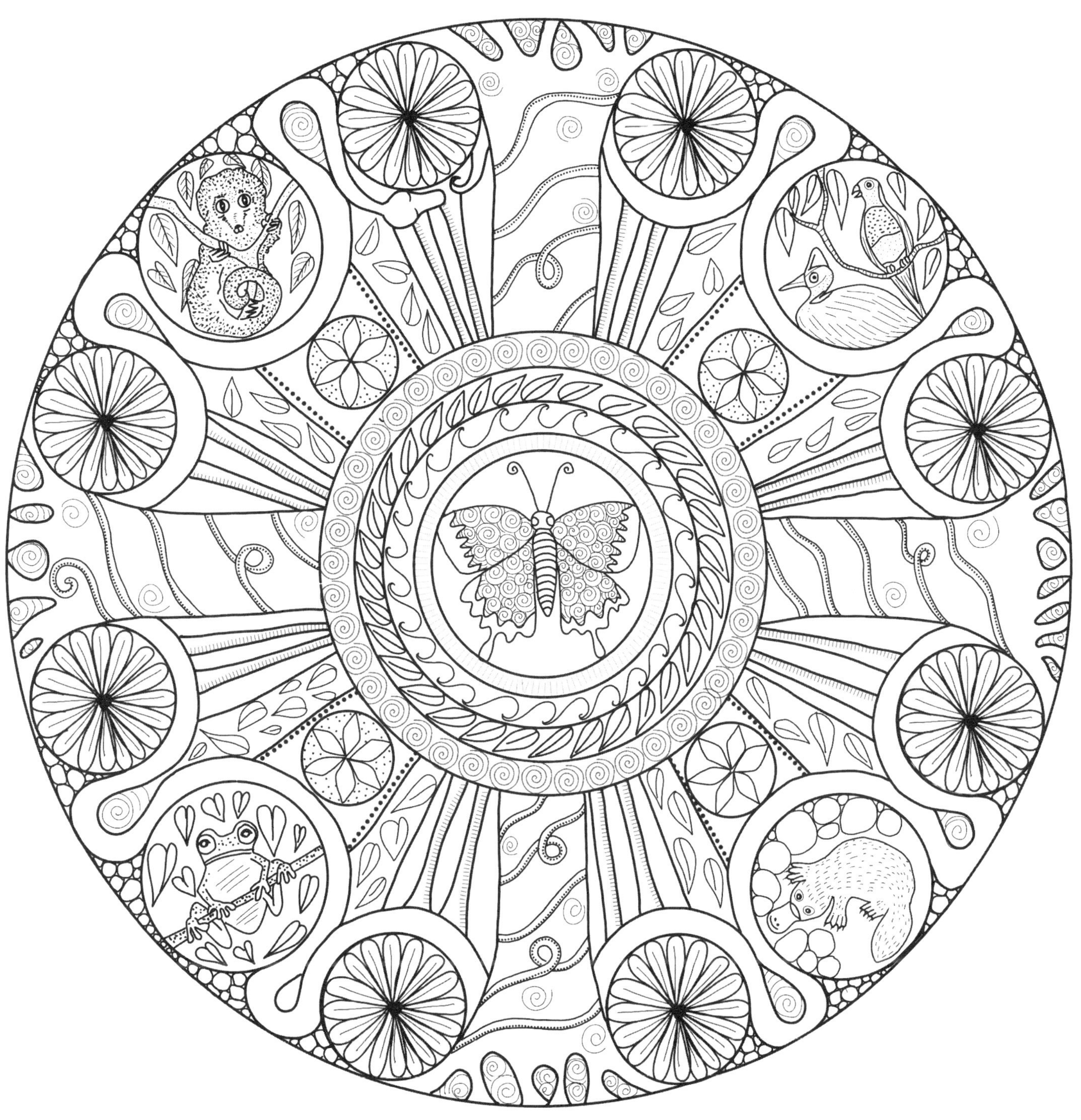

DESERT

◆

Color was important in creating this mandala. I used deep red and orange for soil and rocks, a burst of green for grasses and low shrubs and bright blue for the sky. The sun at the center of the mandala is surrounded by wildflowers and the red of the earth. There are small rocks and stones around the smaller circles, which show some of the wildlife and vegetation found in the Australian desert. Two serpents coil around the night sky in the mandala's axis to bring day and night together. The rocks around the edge reinforce the feeling of the desert.

Wax-based pencils, gouache and oil pastels on paper 50 x 50cm

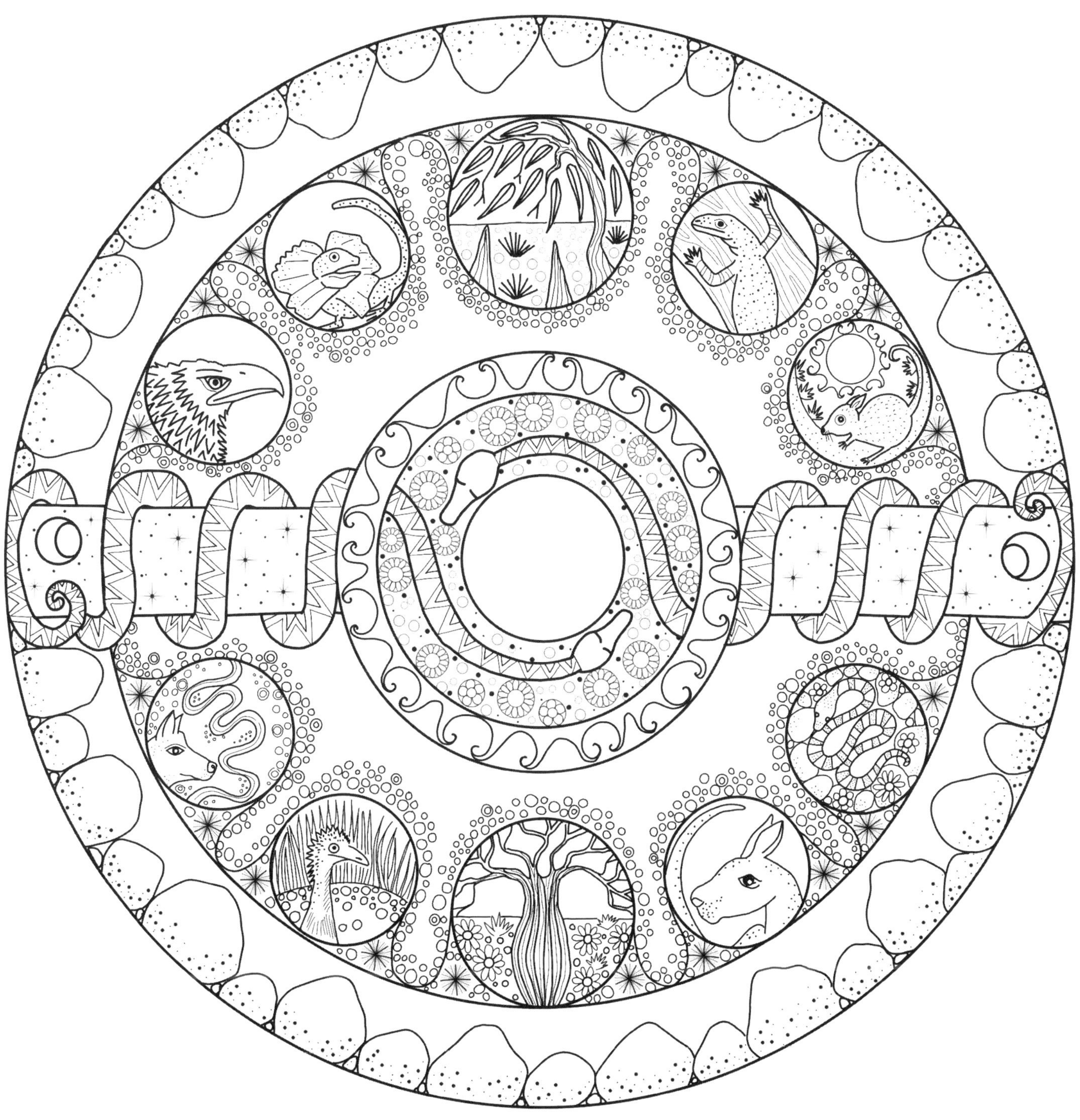

OCEAN

This mandala is my favorite of the landscape series. There is an ocean scene with the sun shining at the center, surrounded by yellow sand. The next circle is life underwater with corals, shells, vegetation and sea creatures. The outer edge is a border of waves and sand. The colors in this mandala were bright and joyful.

Wax-based pencils, gouache and oil pastels on paper 50 x 50cm

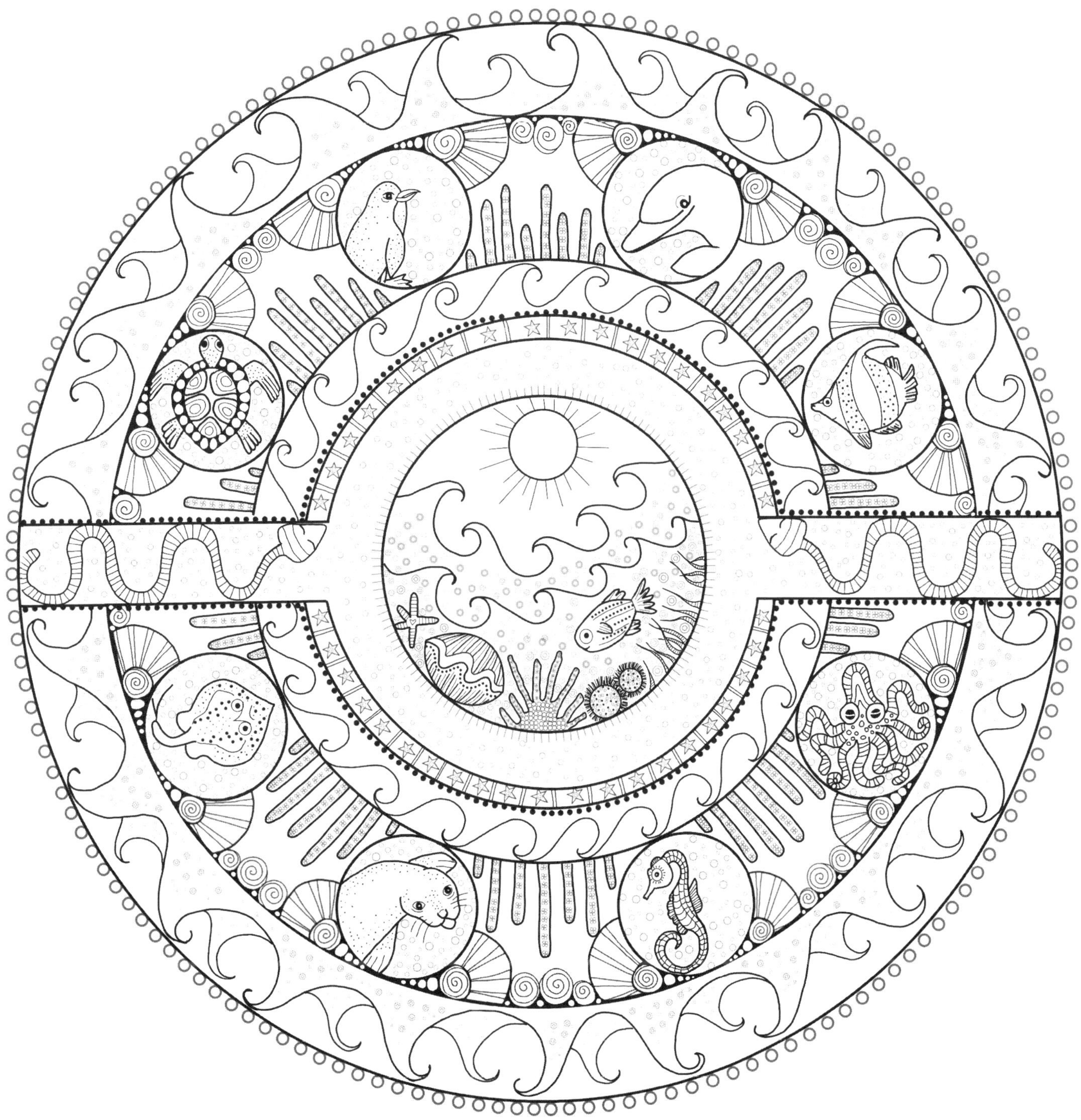

THE FROG PRINCE

◆

The story of the Frog Prince is told through all the images separated by lotus flowers in the middle circle. The outer edge represents the pond where the princess' golden ball falls.

The angel holding the moon over the sleeping princess has hair that becomes the pond, tying the mandala together. This was a lovely mandala to make and an excellent example of how you can weave an entire theme together to create a story.

Wax-based pencils, gouache and oil pastels on paper 50 x 50cm

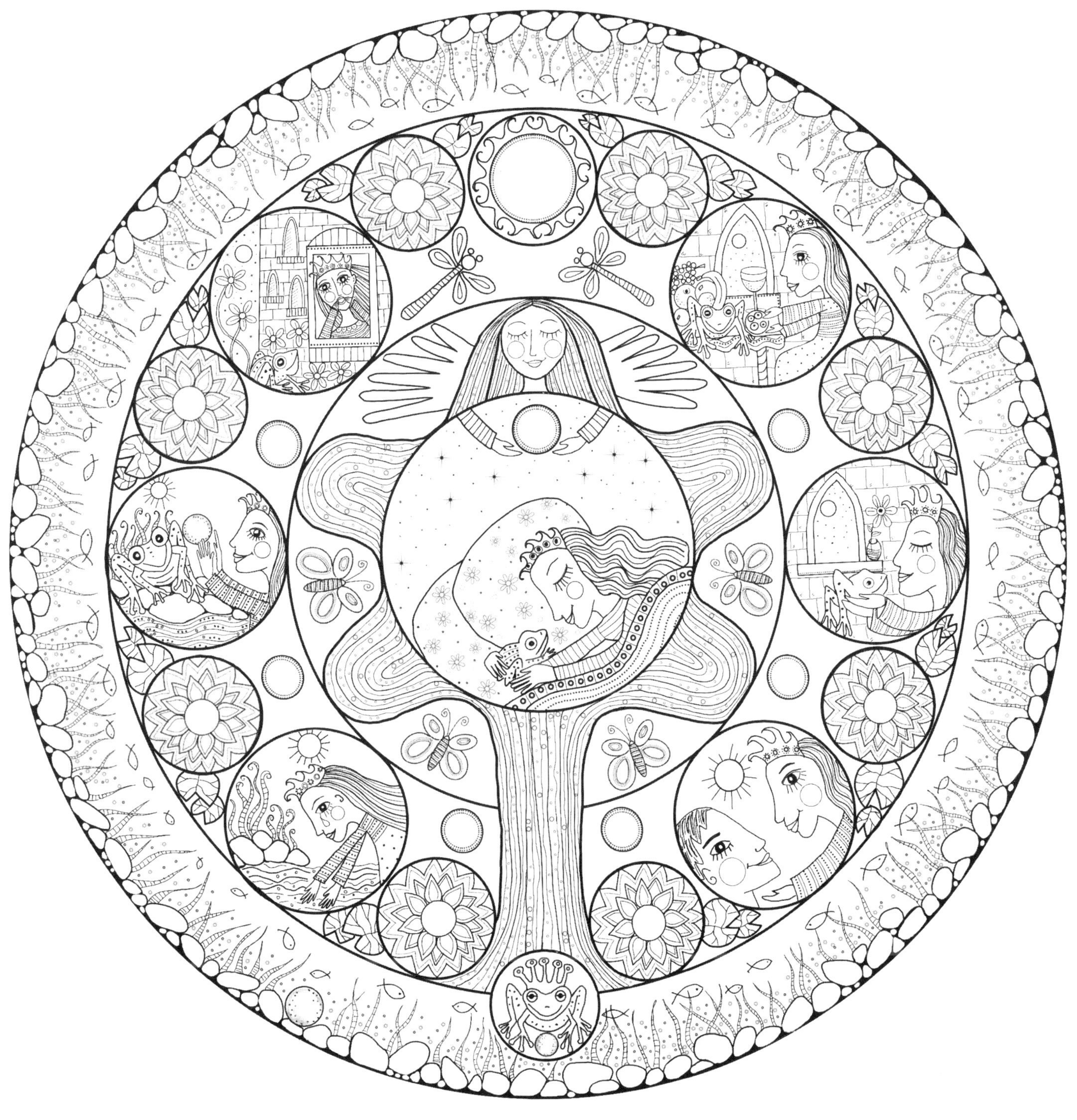

RAPUNZEL

◆

Rapunzel's lovely long hair flows through this mandala to tie the
story together. Another mandala that I enjoyed creating.

Wax-based pencils, gouache and oil pastels on paper 50 x 50cm

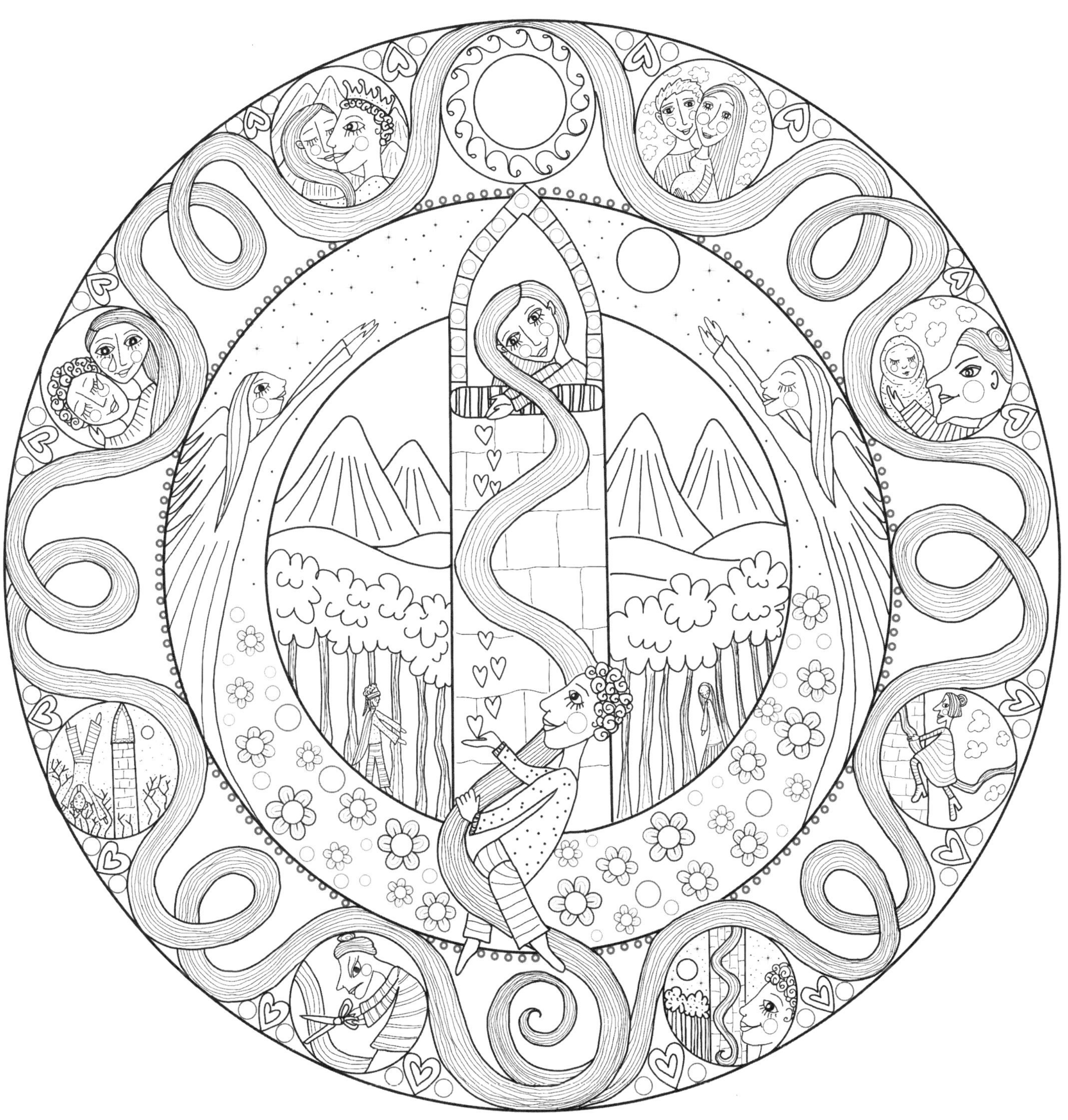

SNOW WHITE

◆

With *Snow White*, I wanted to create more intensity than the other mandalas in this series. This was done using deep reds and brown through the mandala's structure. The trees are close together to give the feeling of a forest, and the apples on the outer edge are side by side to make the mandala feel more contained. Once again, the whole story of Snow White is relayed through the mandala.

Wax-based pencils, gouache and oil pastels on paper 50 x 50cm

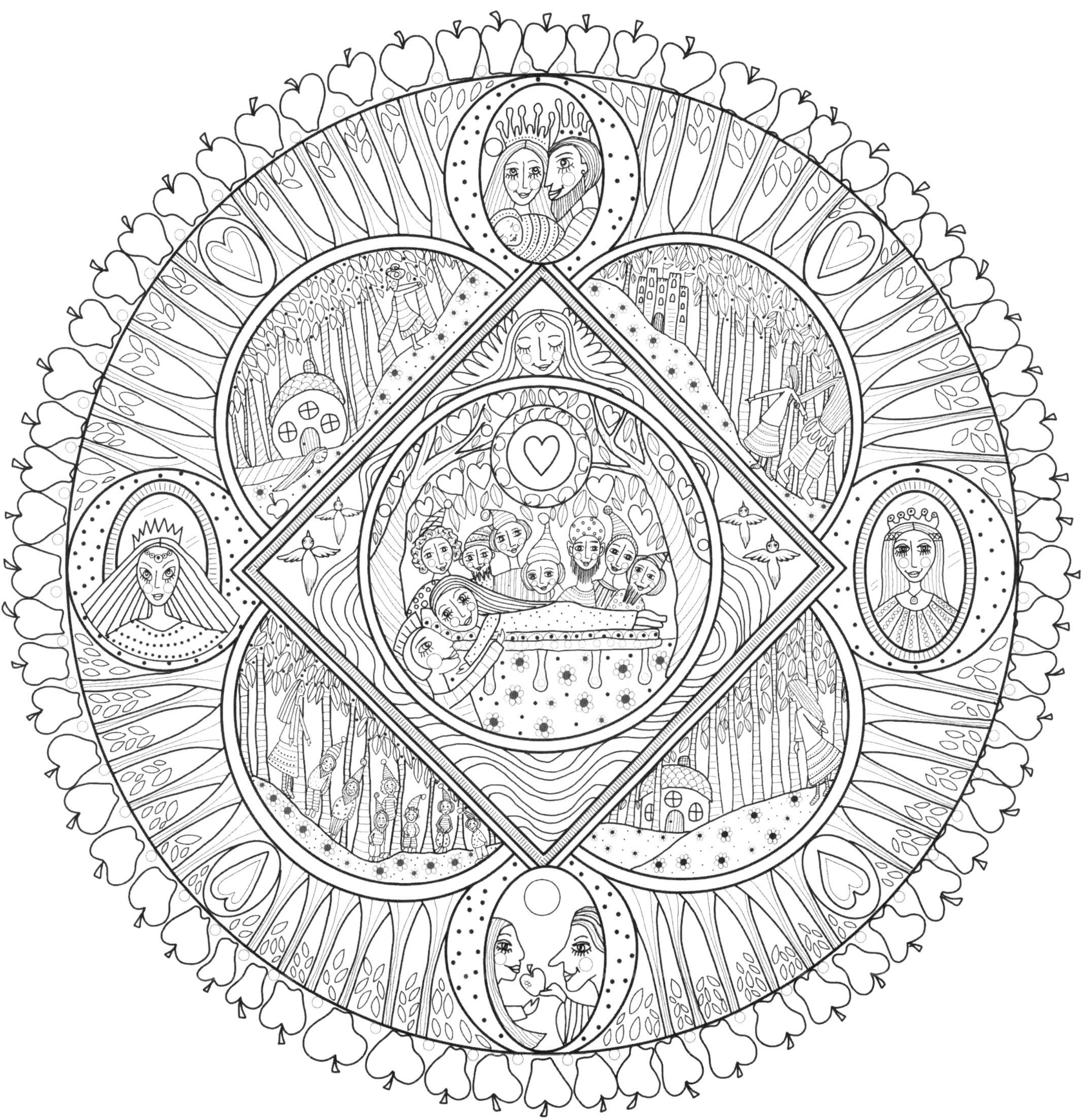

THE FOOL

◆

The Fool takes a leap of faith and steps out into the unknown. In this instance, innocence protects. The girl in the center has elephant ears and a trunk connecting her to Ganesha, the elephant-headed Hindu god known for wisdom and innocence. *The Fool* represents optimism, fresh starts, and fearlessness. The smaller images reveal that you may not know the path ahead, but you can go anywhere if you dive in and follow your heart without expectation.

Wax-based pencils, gouache and oil pastels on paper 25 x 25cm

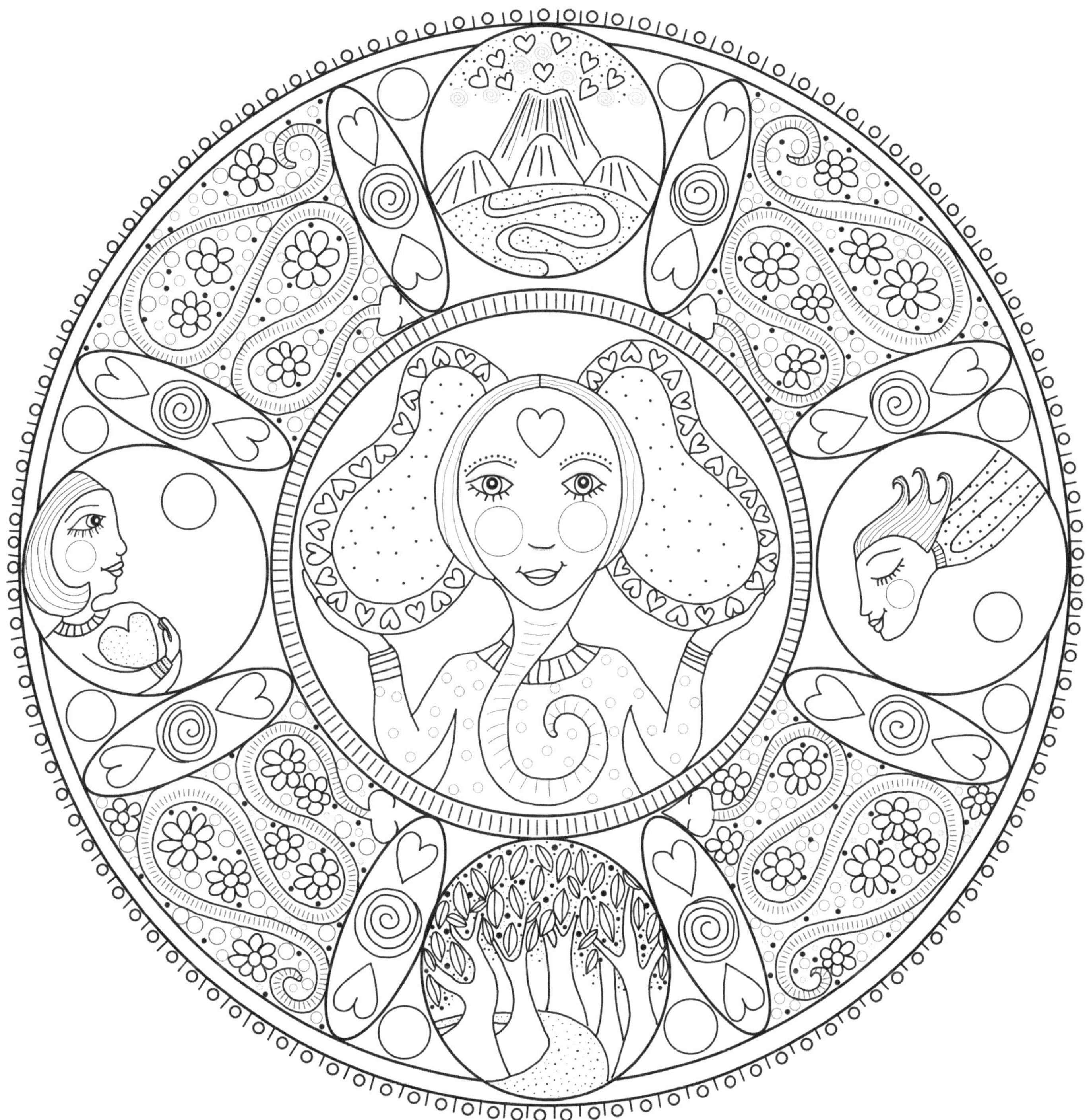

THE MAGICIAN

◆

The Magician represents inspired action and is a conduit between Heaven and Earth. He links creative and practical powers from Source and applies them to the material world. He is consciously aware, focused and committed to his cause. The elements of fire, earth, air and water are included in this mandala. The sun is at his heart, earth beneath his body, sky above him and water surrounding him. At his disposal are tools for accessing emotions (cups), practical solutions (coins), clarity (swords) and energy or action (wands).

Wax-based pencils, gouache and oil pastels on paper 25 x 25cm

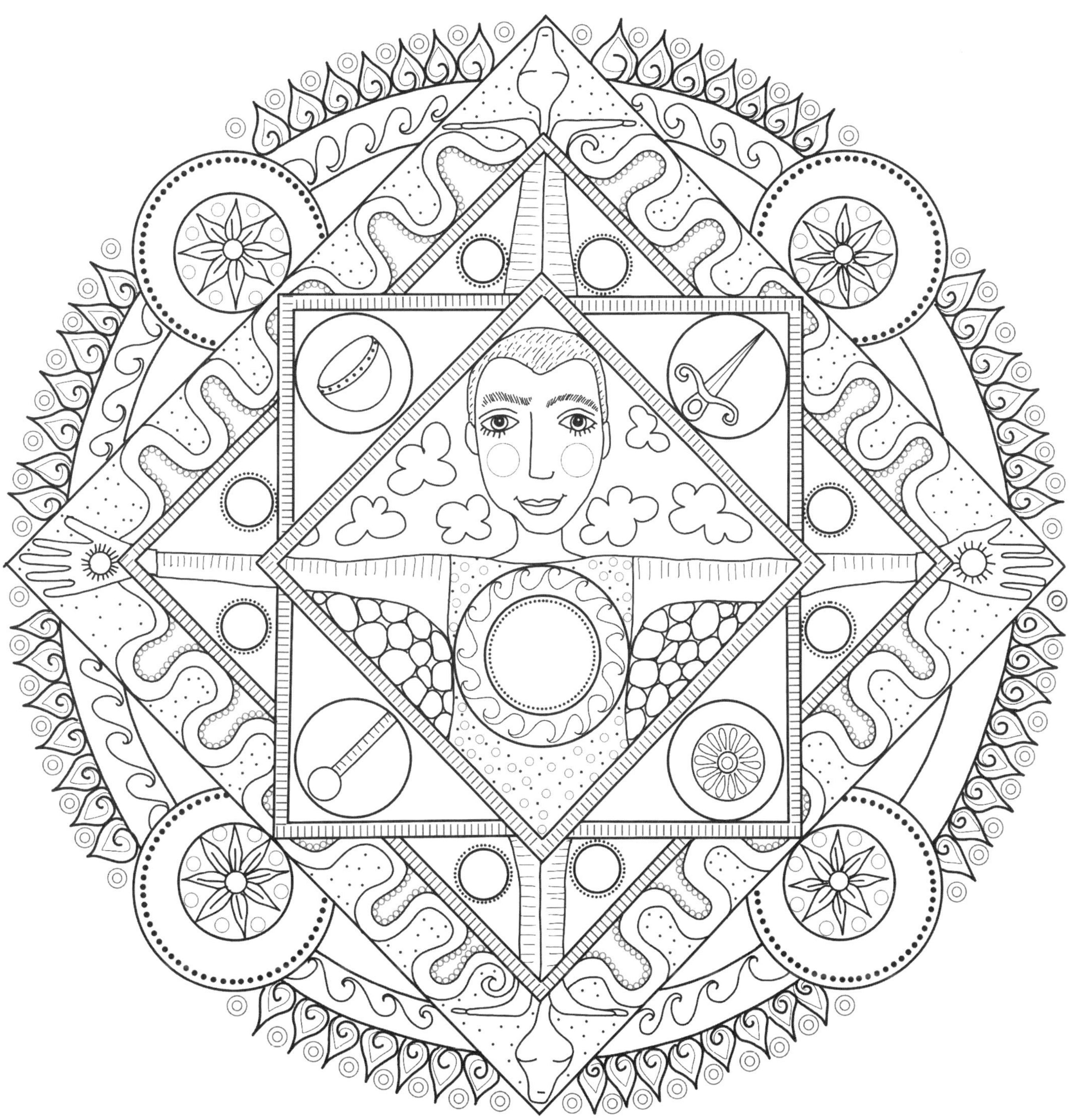

THE HIGH PRIESTESS

◆

The High Priestess operates in the unseen world. She is deeply intuitive, perceptive and open to dreams and imagination. She has her hands in the water, illustrating how she taps into the unconscious world. The water element around the edge of the mandala echoes this, as do the stars, planets and moon in the night sky. To the sides of the High Priestess is a girl with the sun and a girl with the moon. They represent consciousness, subconsciousness and the flow between the two. A serpent with its single eye open weaves through the mandala and connects to the High Priestess' crown chakra, showing her affinity with her inner self and other worlds.

Wax-based pencils, gouache and oil pastels on paper 25 x 25cm

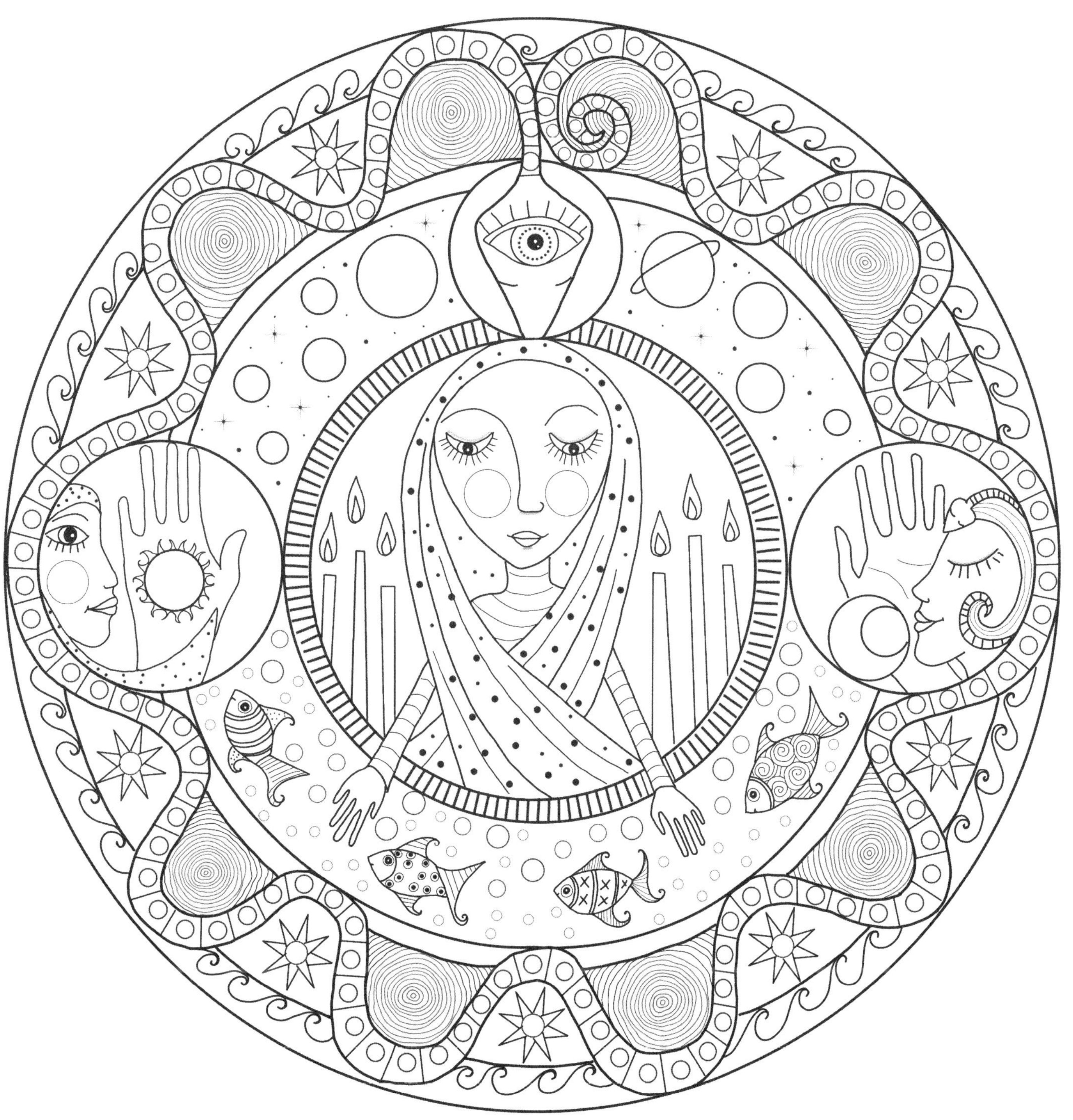

THE EMPEROR

◆

The Emperor represents order, control, stability and authority.
This is reflected in the conformity and rigidness of the mandala.
A father figure and a guiding force, *The Emperor* represents
rules, regulations and leadership. He is seated on a throne with
a lion at his feet to show strength and capability. The mountains
behind him reinforce his strength, as do the stones around the
edge of the mandala.

Wax-based pencils, gouache and oil pastels on paper 25 x 25cm

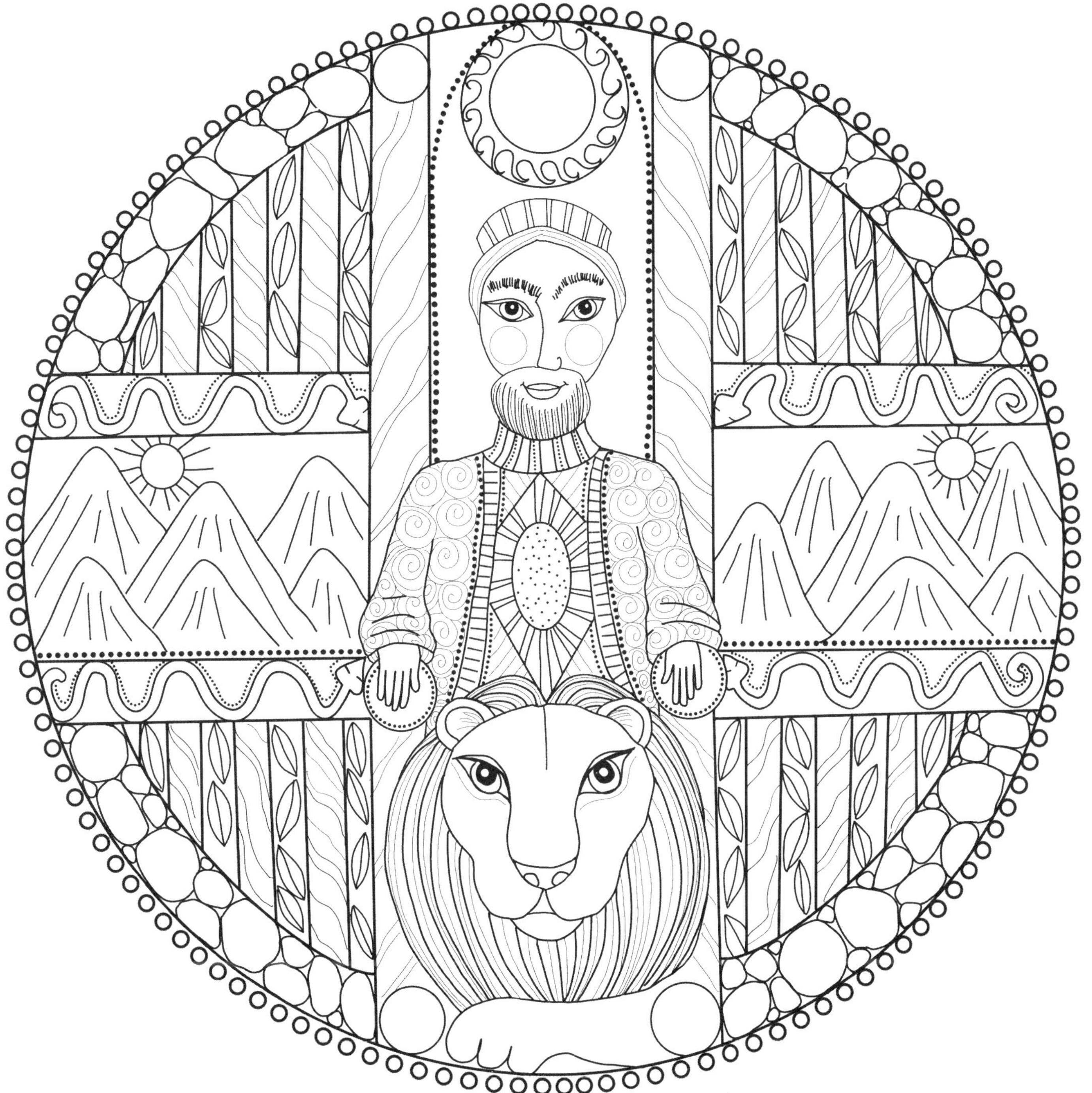

THE EMPRESS

◆

The Empress is the archetypal mother. She represents abundance, wellbeing, fertility and motherhood. She is an all-encompassing loving energy who takes others in with warmth and generosity. The mandala places her at the center of fruit, seeds, flowers, leaves and trees. She is surrounded by earth and nature.

Wax-based pencils, gouache and oil pastels on paper 25 x 25cm

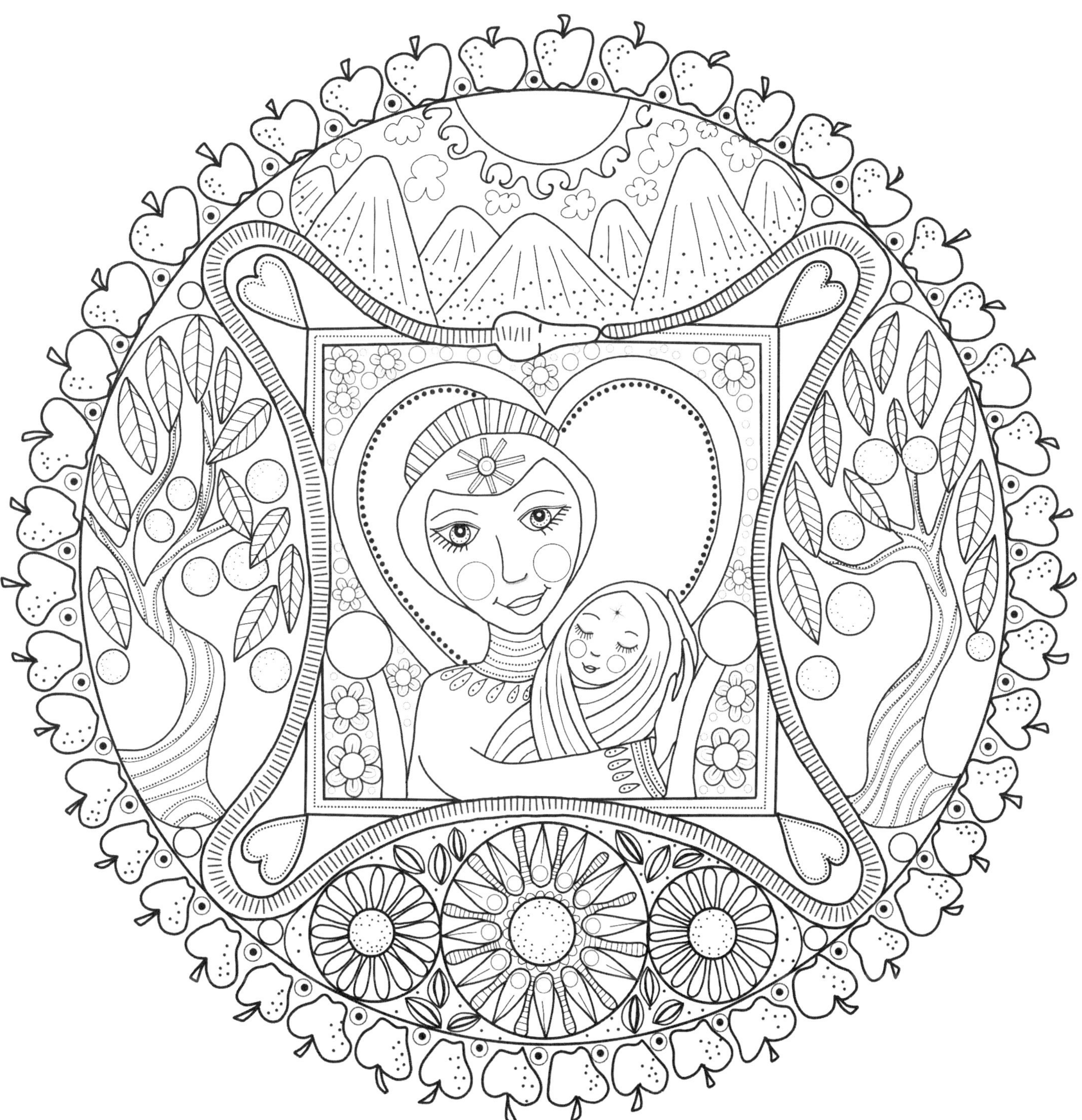

STRENGTH

◆

Strength shows a girl sitting calmly and comfortably on a lion. She has her eyes closed, implying she has no fear of the awake and alert lion. This image is about gentle inner resilience, not force or aggression. *Strength* is about patience, tolerance, compassion and endurance. The square in the mandala reinforces the idea of structure and power, but the surrounding flowers soften this to reflect gentle strength.

Wax-based pencils, gouache and oil pastels on paper 25 x 25cm

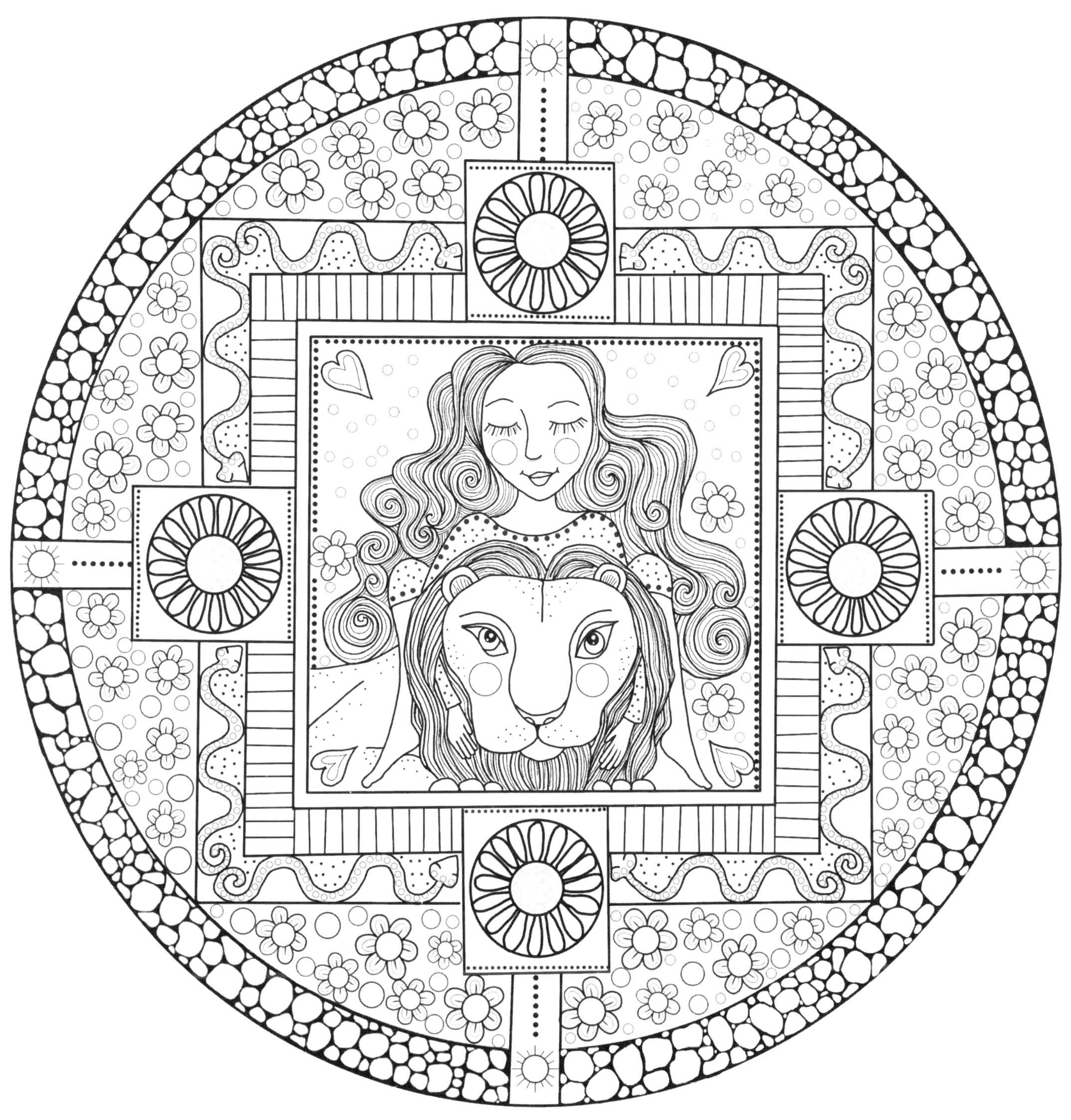

DEATH

◆

Death is about rebirth and transformation, as represented by the serpent in the mandala's center. The girl below, amongst the seeds, is waiting to be reborn. She is reborn above, amongst the flowers — indicating growth from transformation. *Death* symbolizes endings that lead to beginnings and the cycles of life, as seen through the change of seasons. The wolf and the eagle are also connected to these transformations.

Wax-based pencils, gouache and oil pastels on paper 25 x 25cm

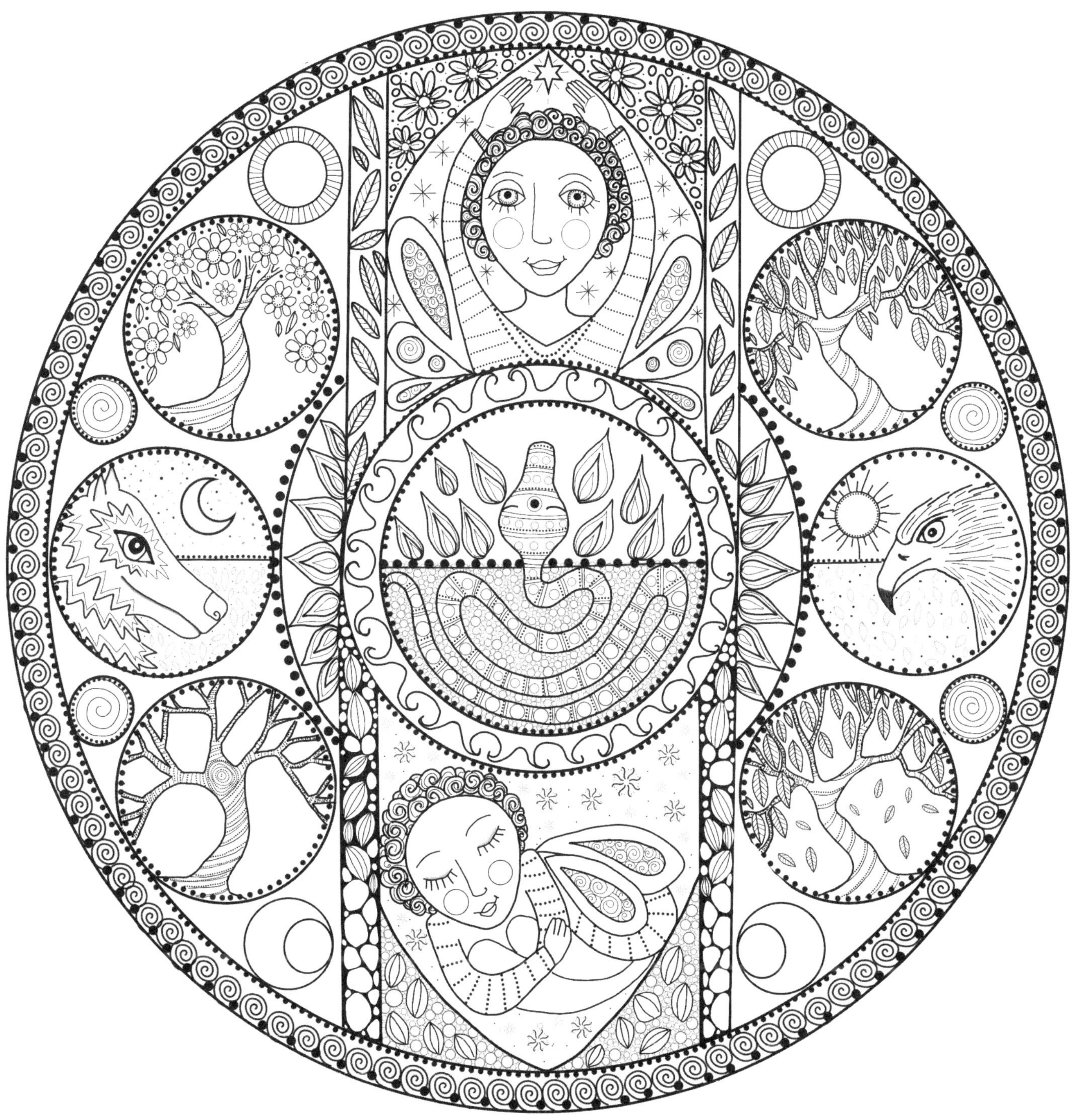

THE HANGED MAN

◆

The Hanged Man represents a time of transition, waiting or being at a crossroads. A pause may be necessary before the next step can be made. This time is for reflection and letting go. *The Hanged Man* can also represent a sacrifice of some sort. In this mandala, the fairy hangs upside-down, waiting while time is suspended on the edges of the mandala. The butterfly wings indicate a transition is underway, and the hearts in the hands symbolize that letting go is part of the transformation process.

Wax-based pencils, gouache and oil pastels on paper 25 x 25cm

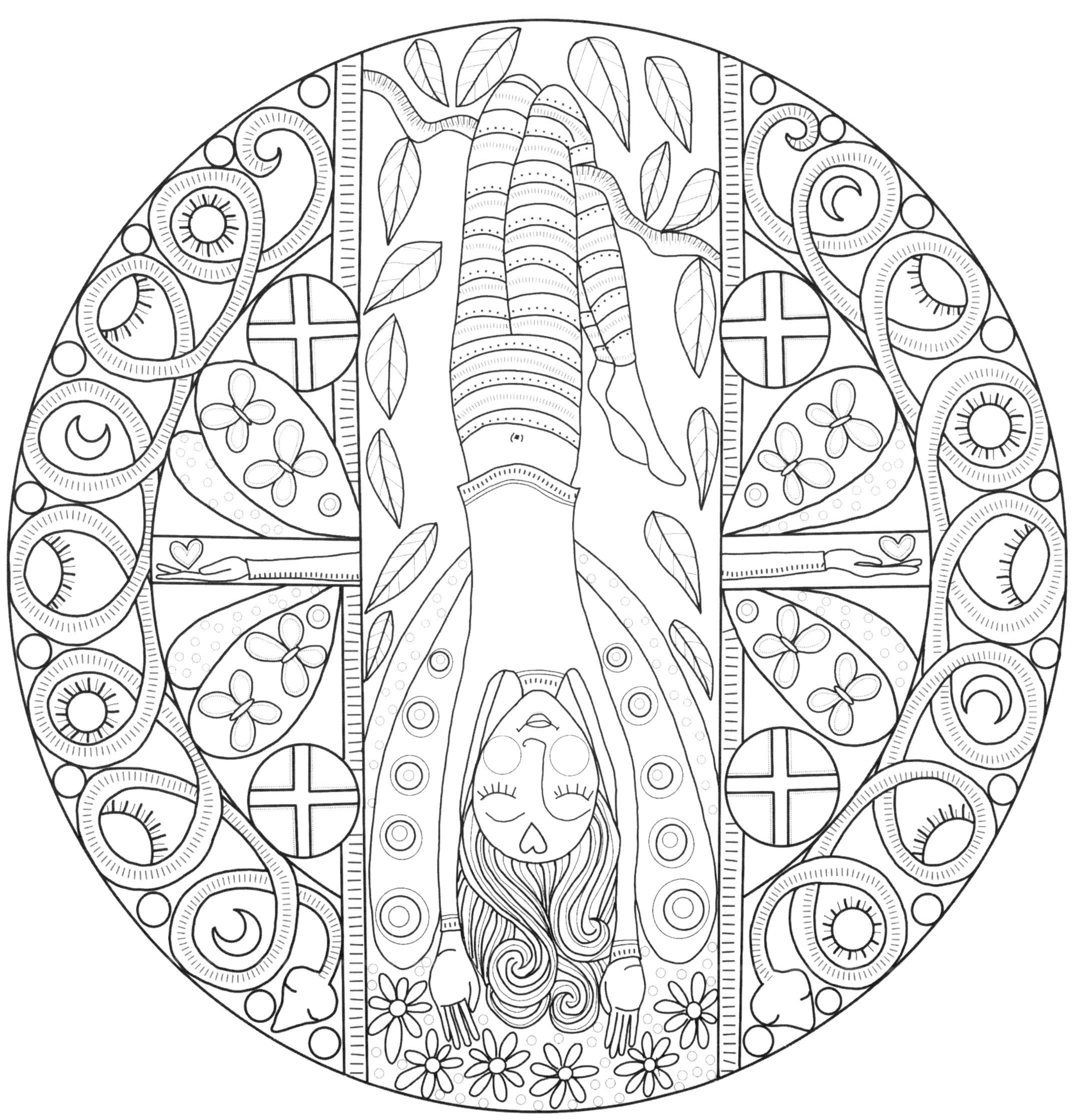

THE THREE OF CUPS

◆

The Three of Cups is a joyful, happy card. It represents celebrations of all kinds, usually with others. In this mandala, the three girls are linked through their cups — which are full. The heart in the center shows their shared happiness and fulfillment. Water and the night sky reinforce the emotional aspect of the suit of cups.

Wax-based pencils, gouache and oil pastels on paper 25 x 25cm

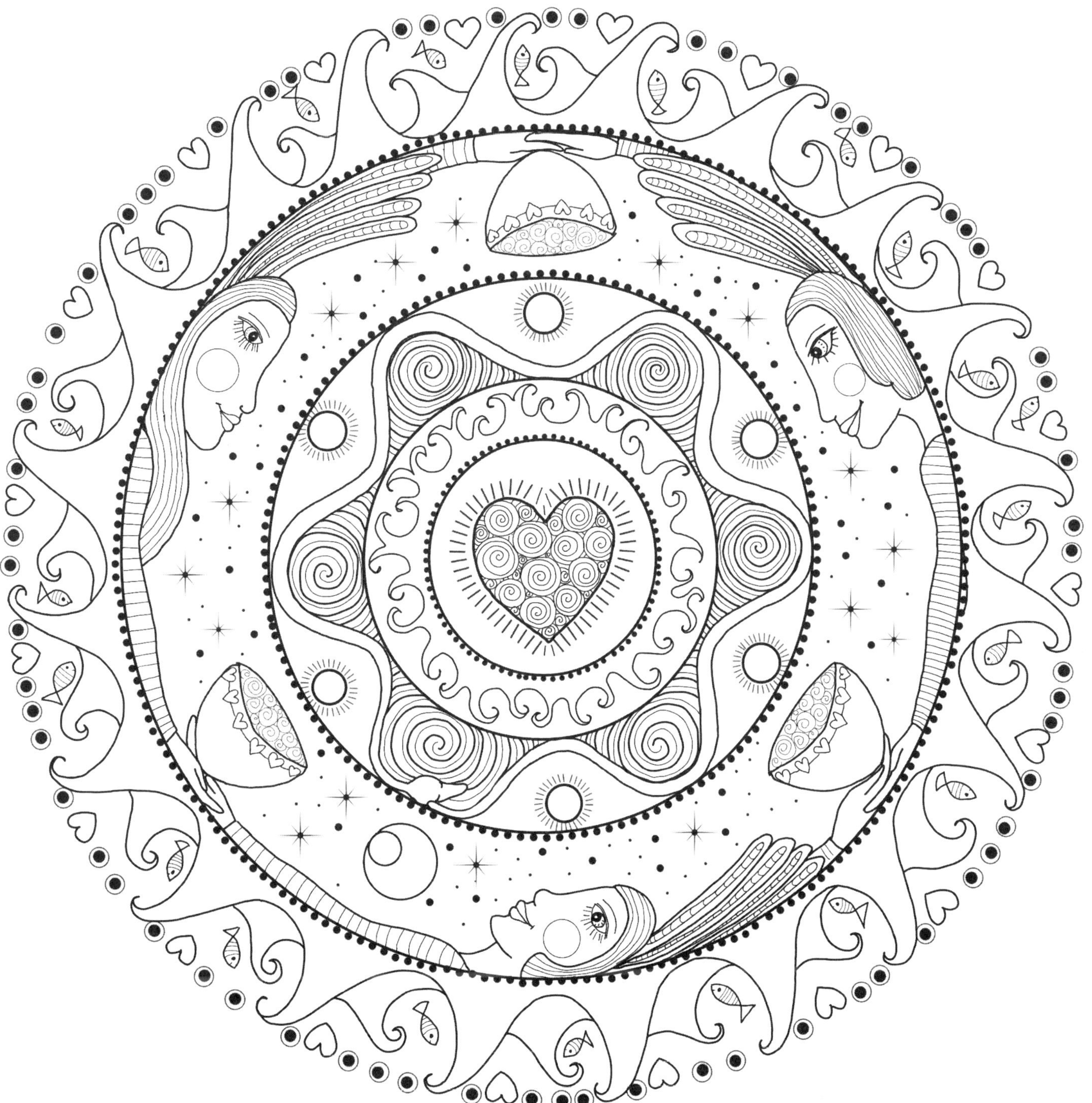

PERSONAL MANDALA 1

◆

A girl and a lion sit in the center, grounded and surrounded by
a heart and a rainbow. The sun shines above a lovely landscape
with trees forming an arch over a backdrop of rolling hills.
Flowers, a river and river stones below, with the presence of
many animals. Spiritual figures are watching from the sides with
the ocean all around them.

Wax-based pencils, gouache and oil pastels on paper 50 x 50cm

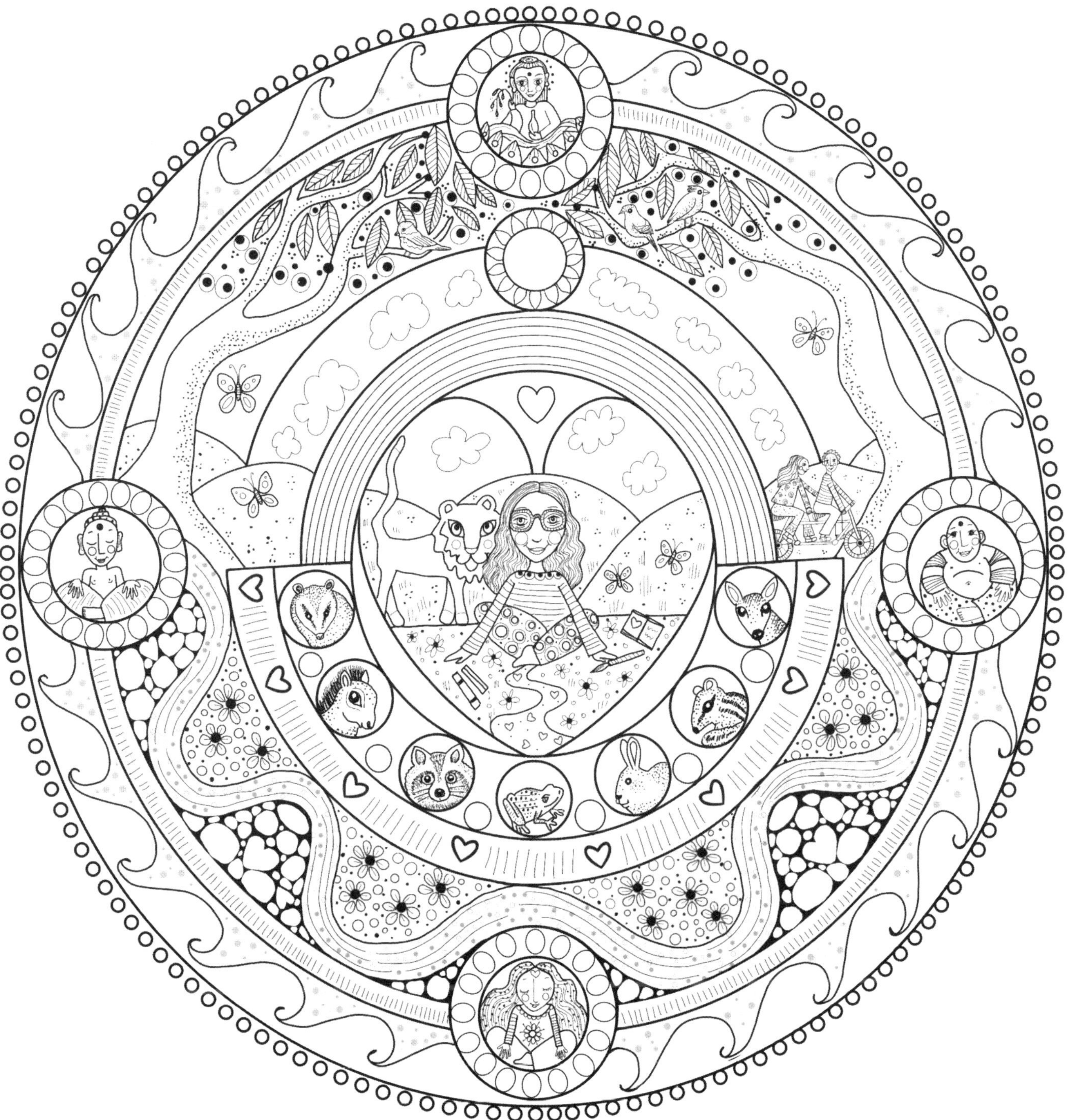

PERSONAL MANDALA 2

◆

A couple and their baby by the fire, a river and two protective
trees. A tiger, a hippo and a kookaburra are watching. Mythical
characters—a unicorn, a dragon, pixies and a goddess—join in.
A river and its stones surround all.

Wax-based pencils, gouache and oil pastels on paper 50 x 50cm

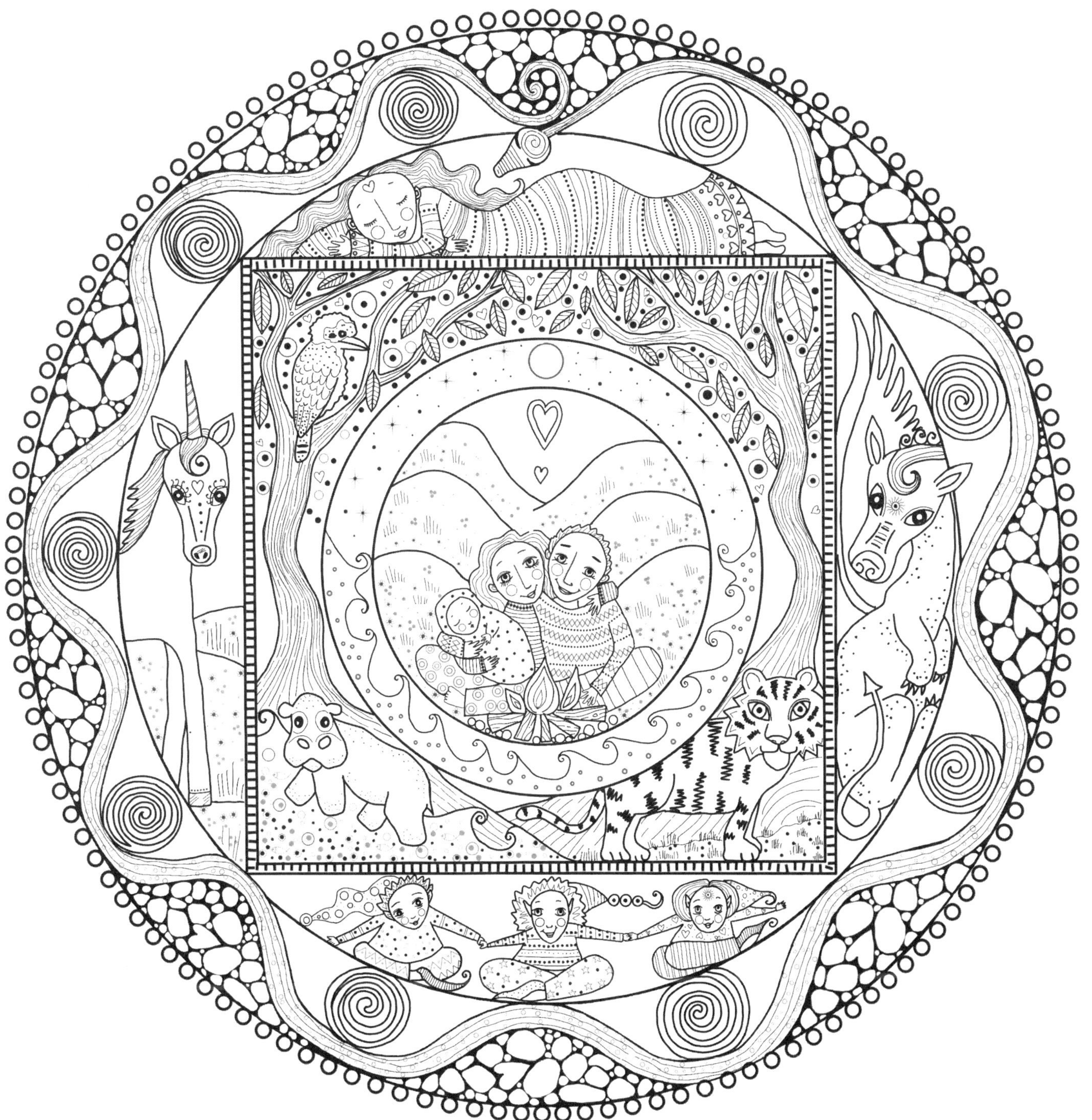

PERSONAL MANDALA 3

◆

A mandala of a couple, peaceful in the landscape. Surrounded by the night sky, mountains, forest, rivers, sunflowers and the sea. Two cats keep them company, and an angel watches over them from above.

Wax-based pencils, gouache and oil pastels on paper 50 x 50cm

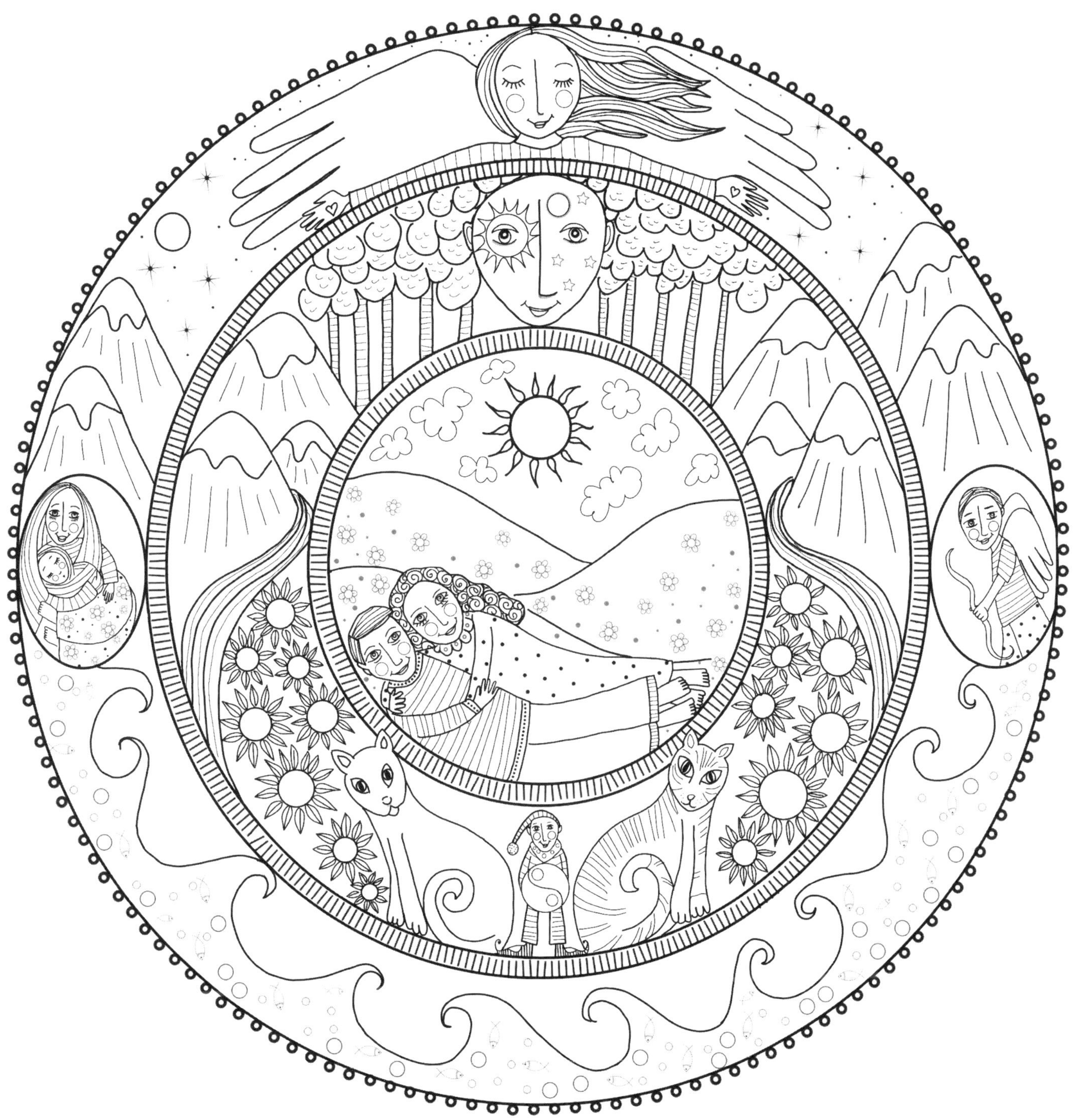

PERSONAL MANDALA 4

◆

A tree spirit connects to a personal landscape. The tree grows
tall toward the mountains behind them, and its roots go
deep into the earth. The sun encompasses the scene that is
surrounded by desert, ocean, mountains and the night sky.

Wax-based pencils, gouache and oil pastels on paper 50 x 50cm

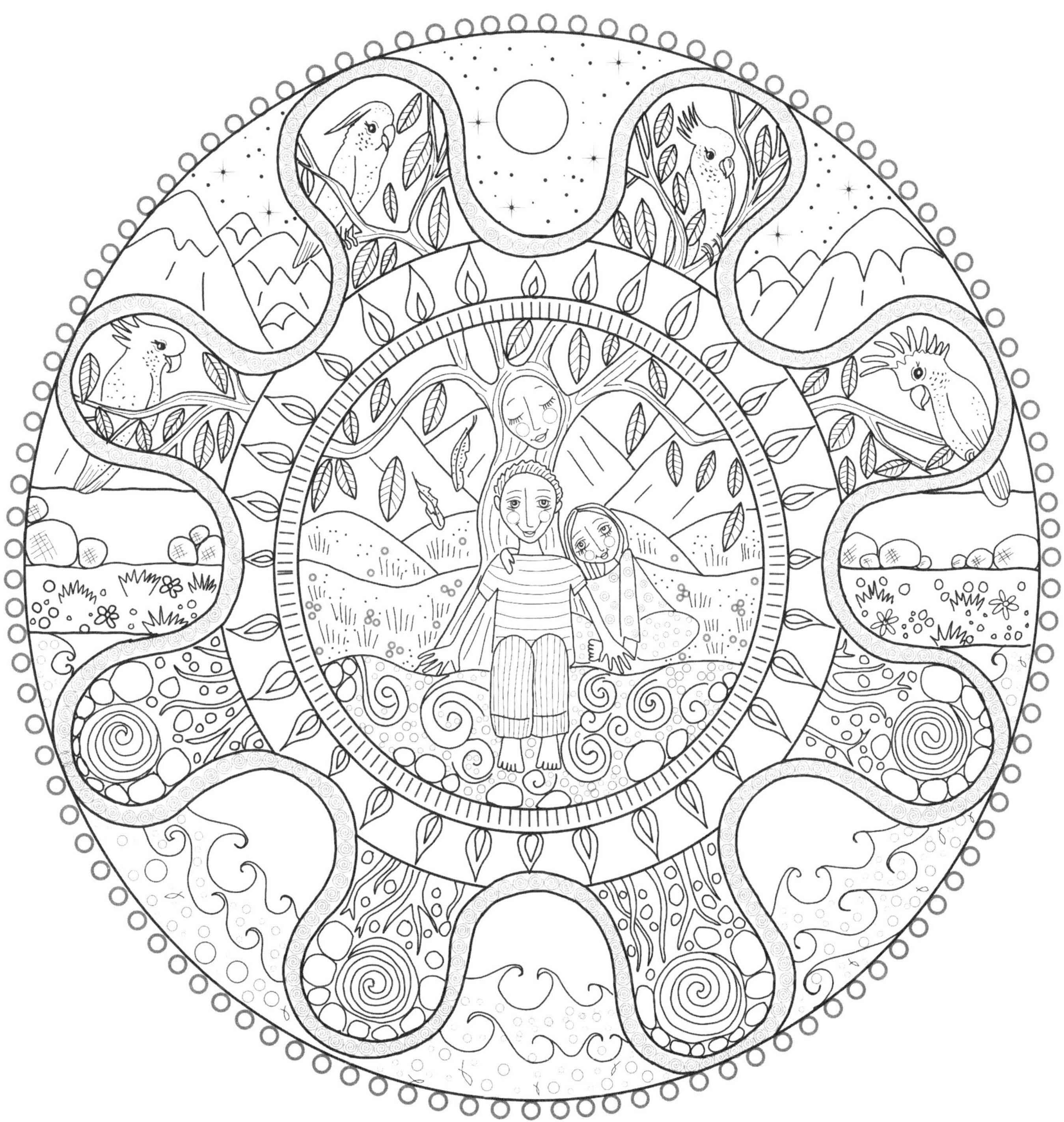

PERSONAL MANDALA 5

A family full of joy delights in a lovely sunny day. Above them,
two angels of the night sky emerge from the mountains.
The scene is held in harmony and flow as depicted by the
Buddha and the dolphins.

Wax-based pencils, gouache and oil pastels on paper 35 x 35cm

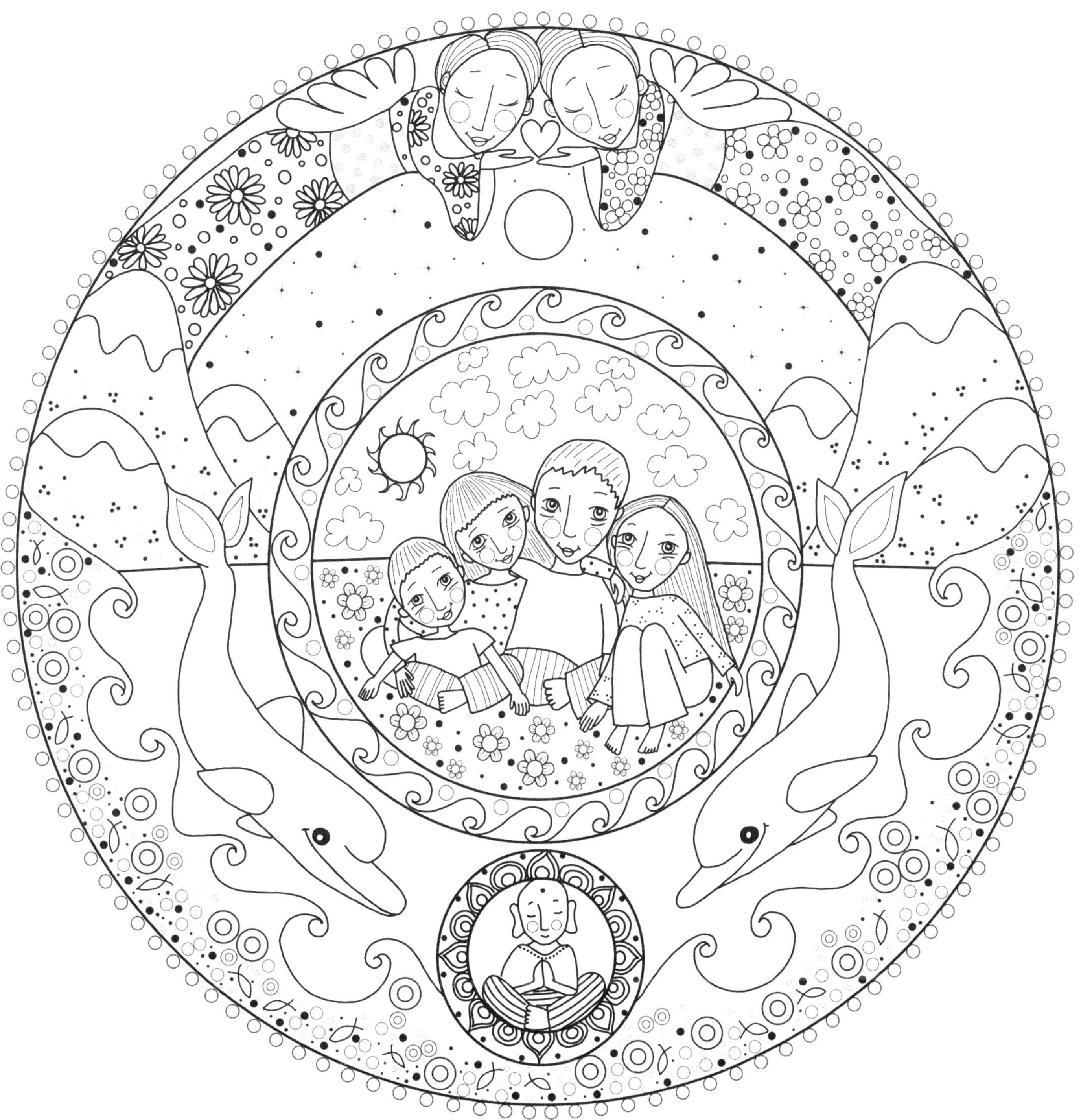

PERSONAL MANDALA 6

◆

A family sits together beneath a tree with the sun radiating
behind them. Flowers, mountains and the sea surround them,
and lots of little animals are looking on. The moon and night sky
are in the far background. The mandala is wrapped in a border of
beautiful petals, much like a lotus.

Wax-based pencils, gouache and oil pastels on paper 35 x 35cm

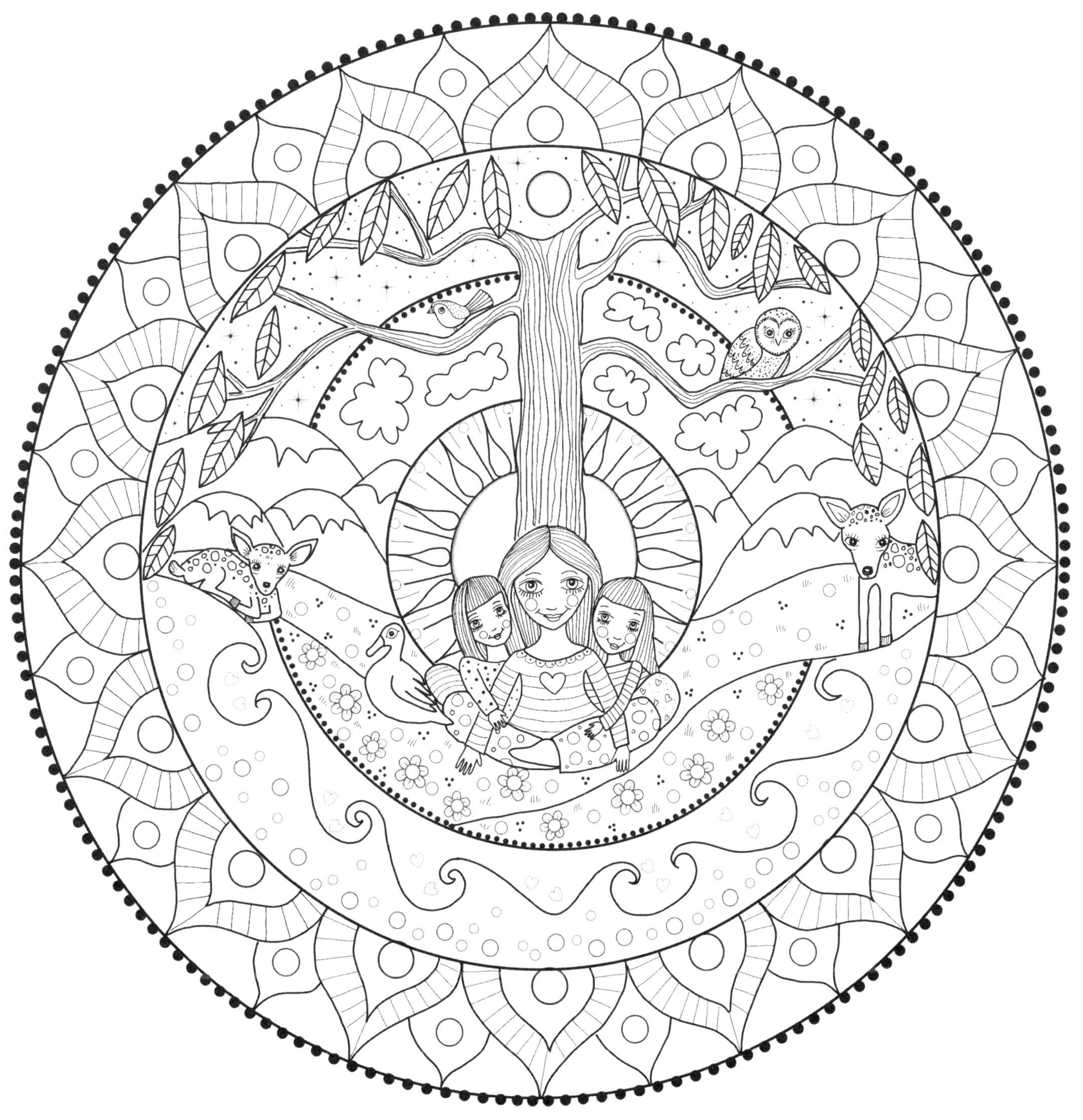

PERSONAL MANDALA 7

◆

The figure in the center of this mandala holds the world in their
hands. This person loves to travel across oceans and deserts.
There is a temple behind for them to aspire to, and the dragons
and a golden sun protect them.

Wax-based pencils, gouache and oil pastels on paper 35 x 35cm

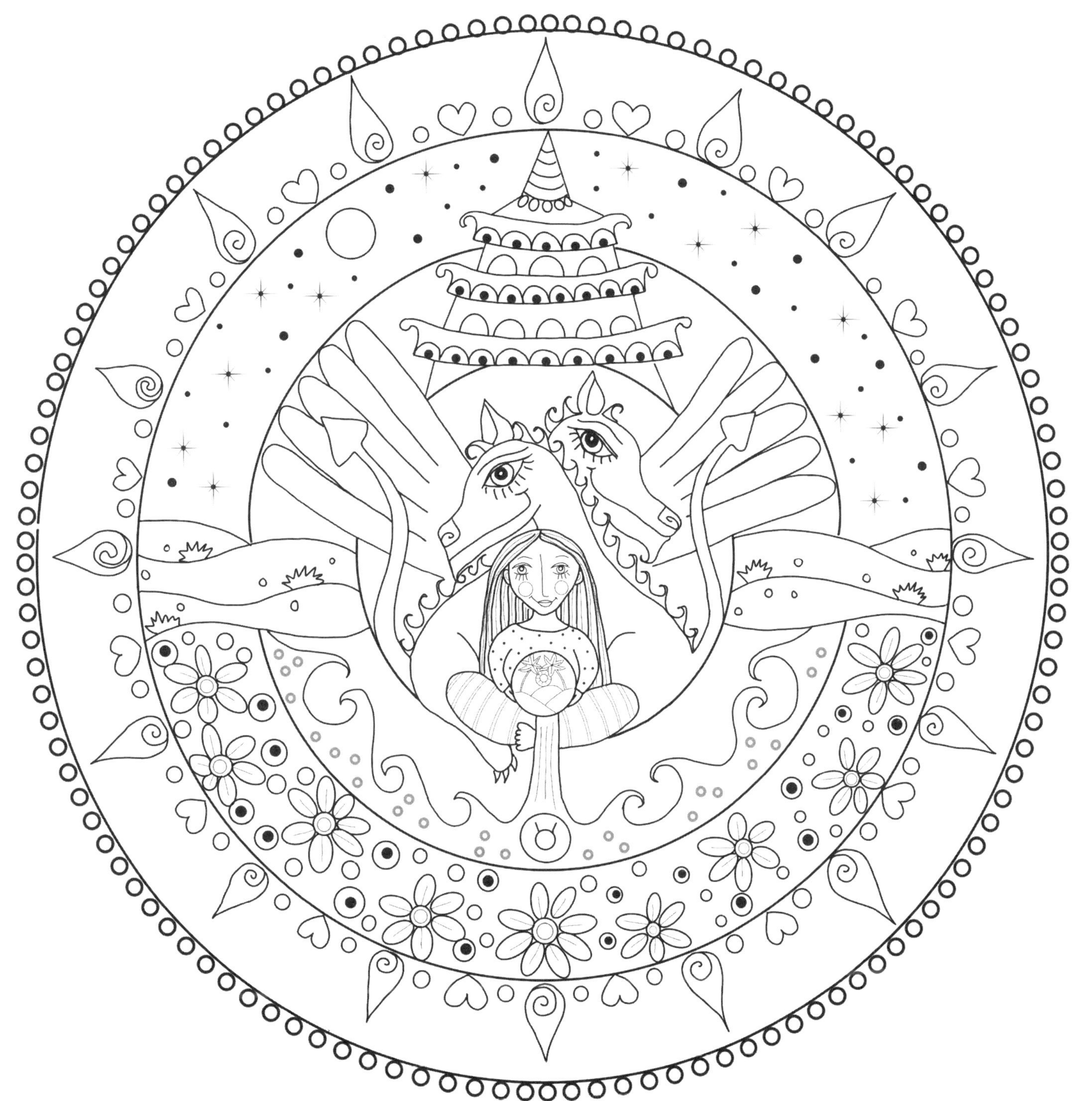

PERSONAL MANDALA 8

◆

A girl who loves to cook and her cat are at home surrounded
by the ocean, friends and flowers. An angel and a magpie
watch over them. The hearts represent the love that emanates
from the home.

Wax-based pencils, gouache and oil pastels on paper 25 x 25cm

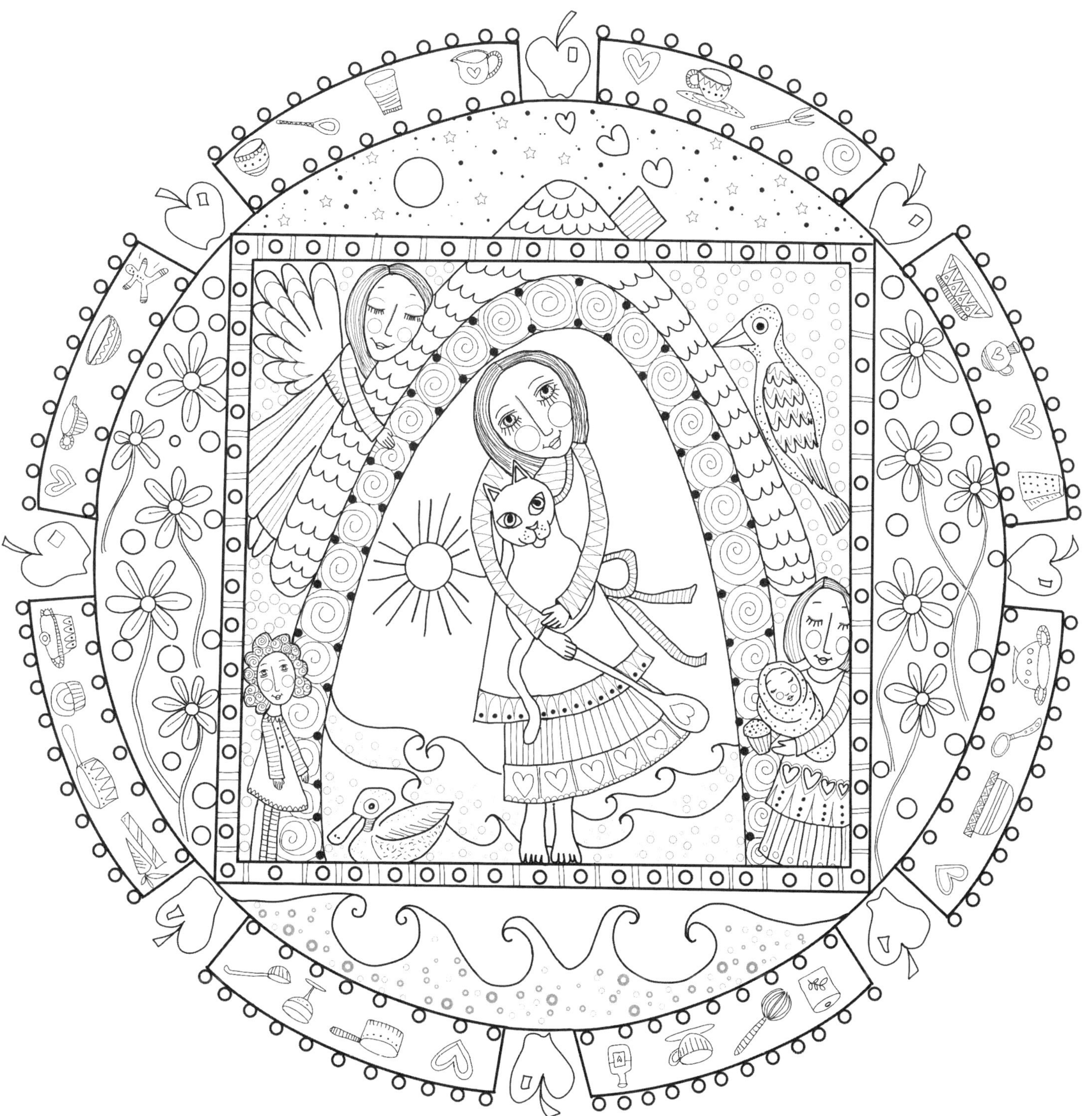

About
LINDY LONGHURST

Lindy Longhurst is an artist and illustrator based in New South Wales, Australia. She has a background in landscape architecture and has been creating art since 1999 and a full-time artist since 2005. Lindy draws inspiration from her strong connection to the earth and nature and her exploration of conscious and subconscious worlds via dreams and meditation. Her whimsical works can be found in private collections worldwide. Lindy's art is collected by those in the healing professions, children and the young at heart. She has exhibited in Europe and Australia and been published in magazines in Australia and the USA.

www.lindylonghurst.com

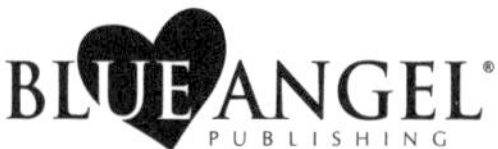

For more information on this or
any Blue Angel Publishing® release,
please visit our website at:

www.blueangelonline.com